THE DEMON GAME

THE DEMON GAME

THE DRUG TAKERS BIBLE

LJ ROBERTS

authorHOUSE®

AuthorHouse™ UK Ltd.
1663 Liberty Drive
Bloomington, IN 47403 USA
www.authorhouse.co.uk
Phone: 0800.197.4150

Published by AuthorHouse 08/21/2014

ISBN: 978-1-4969-8796-9 (sc)
ISBN: 978-1-4969-8797-6 (e)

CONTENTS

VIRGIN

This may bring light to just one,
This may be an answer to some,
This may be a warning for what you are about to become.
I am about to take you on a roller coaster of emotions
that has been my life & all its fears,
21 years of drug abuse has brought with it its fair share
of loneliness depression addiction happiness hope
but most of all painful empty shed tears.
If your mind is a virgin to the demon game what I am
about to write will make you think I am insane,
If your mind is not a virgin to the demon game what you are about
to read will sound oh to familiar just basic everyday plain.
For what I am about to write does not come
from the world of fairy tales or fiction,
What u r about to read is very true & it comes
from the painful world of drug addiction.

WHAT

What is it that allows us to feel such strong emotions as happy or sad,
& what is it that stops us from switching them off
when all there doing is driving us mad.
What is it that brakes & lets things to get so out of control,
What is it that brakes & allows even the
smallest things in2 destroy your soul.
What is it in your head that allows things to become so very wrong,
What at this point makes inside you no longer feel strong.
What is it that allows you to go so far of the rails,
What is it that stops you getting back on allows all your attempts 2 fail.
What is it that allows you to feel so mentally & physically week,
What is it that is cutting of the strength you
once had when you were at your peak.
What is this thing that is taking your very life away,
What is this thing that is getting stronger every hour of everyday.
What is this thing that is beginning to take over your body mind & soul,
What is this powerful thing that is dragging
your life towards that black hole.
What is this thing that is taking out the good
& in its place adding more dark strife,
What is this thing that has took control of the destiny of your life.
What is this thing that is taking your life & it's very light away,
What is this thing that has dug deep in2 your head & is here to stay.
What is this thing that has put you & your life in a fight
2 the death put you in a situation of do or die,
What is this thing that made you so scared all you
can do is sit alone in a dark room & cry.
Why is this thing saying it's something you cannot beat
& either way your head will never be the same,
What if I was to tell you welcome to
THE DEMON GAME...............

IN THE BEGINNING

Its 1991 I am only 12 years old I decide to try my first drug,
So innocent yet still a stupid little mug.
At the time I must have thought my friends would be
saying lee's the man lee's the one I want to be,
What a stupid little boy if that's as far as I could see.
For the next few years I began to take different
drugs & always a little more,
But it was nothing out of my control I was only taking
so that life wasn't allowed to become a bore.
But just after I turned nineteen I let myself get mislead into an unknown
addiction I could see it was delivering me in2 the demon games hell,
This was something I didn't see coming until it was too late to tell.
Little did I know I was being dropped into the
game & its deadly demons of the night,
Now you are about to read the last fourteen years of myself inflicted fight.

THE TRAP

All I seemed to do was run through a tempting open gate,
Little did I know the games demons were waiting
to shut it & change my life's fate.
All of a sudden I am somewhere I have never been,
Looking around thinking this must b can only b a scary dream.
I didn't know I had fallen in2 the demon games trap taken the bait,
Now God can only look down hoping I am strong
enough 2 change back my life's ever darking fate.
This place I am in seems so strange seems
there's only one direction I can go,
Now wishing I had never come through the gate but how was I to no.
How was I to no running through such a tempting open gate,
Was going to lock me in the demon game where I can see my deaths date.
But still I can't see still I am blind,
The games demons r now free to destroy my mind.

SLIPPING

I don't know what is happing to me everything is
slipping away my life is going downhill,
Now the only relief I get is when I swallow the demon pill.
You see when you take the demon pill for a
while all your troubles go away,
The demon pill guaranties you it will take away
your troubles for at least another day.
But the demon pill must have seen me coming from a mile away,
I should have seen the addictive demon pill coming
I should have known to turn the other way.
But now the demon pill has my head exactly where it wants it to be,
It's making me blind the demon pill is the only thing it allows me 2 see.
Now in way too far to try & turn & run away,
Scared without the demon pill I will not be able to face another day.
Now when I try to come of the demon pill
my emotions start running wild,
I can no longer control them because they r no longer weak small or mild.
The demon pill now has all emotional control over me,
The demon pill now's I am only happy when totally out of my tree.
The demon pill is now beginning to drain away my life's light,
Bringing with it the games long dark deadly night.

D. CALLING

I am beginning to straighten up so I'd better
go see if I can find some more,
Can't get no fucker in so how the hell am I suppose to score.
Must stay high because it's the only way I now know,
Think must be a score out there & that's where I must go.
I must not come down because normal life is
something I haven't seen of much,
I once had a normal life but its way 2 far 2 try & touch.
Must stay high so I can stay here floating on cloud 9,
Here my life is hassle free & always seems fine.
I have become so used to being totally fucked out my face,
Now when I am straight my life feels awkward & out of place.
Now always totally wasted haven't got any safe sensible place left 2 go,
Scared of my dark lonely life because normality
is something I no longer know.

THE DEAD OF NIGHT

When you think hard about it the dead of
night is really a scary place 2 be,
Alone with your thoughts & only your thoughts because
through the darkness there is no light 2 see.
Everything dark peaceful & so very quiet,
Day time compared 2 the dead of night is like a riot.
The only noise is from the occasional passing car,
The only light is from that 1 distant solitary star.
The dead of night is when you find out what lies deep inside your head,
All kinds of crazy thoughts running through as
if triggered by something just said.
The only thing braking up my thoughts is the sound of my pen,
My head is doing overtime trapped here with all its
thoughts pouring from its little dark den.
Sitting here in the dead of night with all these 2 many thoughts
I begin 2 see further in2 my head than I first wanted 2 go,
But these thoughts keep racing through my head
it's not like I can stop them by saying no.
I am just going further & further in2 the abyss of things
that r in the deepest darkest realms of my mind,
I don't know why some people say piece & quiet helps them unwind.
I think for me & my thoughts I'd better get away from this dead of night,
I think I'll take my thoughts away from the darkness
2 a place where there is a little more light.
When your mind is being screwed by the demons of drugs
the dead of night can be quite a dark scary place 2 be,
You see further & deeper in2 your head you see
darkness you never wanted 2 see.

SCARED

Now I am scared I know something is wrong
something has definitely gone really bad,
My heart is losing its beat my soul is numb my
thoughts r in an everlasting state of sad.
I keep trying 2 pull out of it I am trying my
hardest 2 cling 2 this unwinnable fight,
But the demons r now so strong & my life is
sliding in2 the dark deadly night.
The demons have grown so strong because thieve
been feeding on my silent cry's of plight,
Demons always grow strong when they know your
life is losing its strength giving light.
Their voices scare me but lately there all I hear,
I don't know it yet but I am losing everything &
everybody that 2 me is close & dear.
The demons no I have become so scared I do anything they say,
They also know I am no longer mentally
strong enough 2 drive them away.
I hear the demons saying there going 2 take my broken battered soul,
Little did I know they'd have 2 kill me first am no good 2 them whole.
Now the only things that do understand me r the demons in my head,
I am exactly where they want me with most of my
friends looking at me as if I am the walking dead.
Now all the people I thought were here 2 help just stand & stair,
Because in my eye's all they can see is the demons glare.

DEADLY DREAMS

Soaked with sweat from another horrific nightmare I awake,
Got such a fright it was like someone stabbing
my heart with a wooden stake.
For months now every night has been the same,
Even my dreams aren't safe from the demons of the game.
I now have at least 2 or 3 panic attacks a night,
To sleep I feel as if I am 3 again & I must leave on the TV & light.
Dreams of terrifying monsters dragging me from my bed,
Waking up in a puddle of sweat not knowing if I am alive or dead.
Dreams of not being able 2 breathe waking up gasping for air,
To resettle myself it takes hours & all I can do is sit & stair.
Dreams of nothing but death blood guts & pain,
Even I have begun to wonder when I am asleep am I 100% sane.
The demons terrorize me when I am asleep scare
the shit out of me when i am awake,
I'd be a lot better of if it wasn't a dream when
they were using that wooden stake.
So now you see when I am unconscious conscious or subconscious
my head doesn't get a break from the demons of the game,
And with every pending night they get worse just
more of the overwhelming evil dark same.

STOLEN EMOTIONS

I am now so emotionally week & all my confidence has long gone,
The demons have engulfed it all making them self's more strong.
But they will give me my confidence back if I give in & do as they say,
Suppose i better get wasted so the demons will give me the
confidence needed 2 make it through another day.
The strong emotions I had that gave me the strength
2 fight the demons engulfed them whole,
Now the only emotions they let me feel r the dark one's
which they are using 2 gain access 2 my soul.
When I am straight I find it hard 2 even look at people in
case they catch a glimpse of the demons in my eyes,
I don't want anyone 2 no so if they ask any questions
I cover my tracks by telling little white lies.
I hate lying but I can't tell them the truth about what is making me sin,
They would never understand they would only think I
should be locked inside the walls of a loopy bin.
Even small tasks in everyday life make me feel on edge & out of place,
Without my good emotions I just feel the whole world is right in my face.
When I go out even just across 2 the shops
it's like everyone is looking at me,
It's like they are staring at something or someone that I can't see.
Even though it makes the pain worse & is steadily wasting me away,
To make it through everyday life I must do as the demons say.
When I do as they say I make it by with
relative ease as easy as it is 2 blink,
But when I am like this it's the demons at my emotional
controls & what they do 2 me I shudder to think.
But the demons r in control of my emotions
& they use them at their wile,
If I don't do what I am told they send an uncontrollable wave of
dark emotions 2 get me back on the powder & demon pill.
The demons just want 2 be the ones with outright emotional control,
They know they're getting ever nearer to gaining possession of my soul.
The demons r saying the end for me is near,
They know all they have 2 do is sit at the emotional controls & steer.

RAIN

Have you ever sat back & watched as a rainy hays rolls
over the landscape getting ever closer 2 you,
That rainy hays is going 2 come overhead you
can't stop it no matter what you try 2 do.
Well in my life it's raining & things don't look 2 good,
Could be something 2 do with far 2 many drugs not enough sleep or food.
I am looking around & everything in my life
is disappearing in2 this rainy hays,
It seems such a long time ago when life was full of sunny rays.
Sitting here in this rainy hays thinking of good times from my past,
Realizing in this present any good can never last.
Everything in my life right now is blighted by self inflicted grief & pain,
Knowing that the demons of drugs have taken any chance
of me ever returning 2 a life of relative plane.
Through this rainy hays I can still see a tiny bit of life's
beauty but on my eyes it puts a heavy strain,
To try & reach back I am no longer strong enough because
inside me I have forgot how 2 fight the pain.
I know if I was 2 try & reach back 2 life's beautiful plain,
I would have 2 go through the demons that have
just destroyed me put out my life's flame.
It's as if the demons used this rainy hays 2 bring
2 my life these endless dark days,
They broke me away from my strength within the pack
& lead me out in2 the week 1 of wondering strays.
Looking around as the rain turns the green grass 2 black muds,
The demons no 2 get 2 my soul all they have 2 do is stay in my blood.
This rainy hays is now so big I don't know if I
will see the time when it will pass,
Getting bigger & bigger its now just a huge life engulfing dark mass.
This rainy hays has now consumed what was left of the fading light,
Scared weak & alone I must face the demons games black deadly night.

 BLACK NIGHT

With the fading light turning 2 an everlasting dark night,
The demons have taken so much life out of
me I feel I am fading out of sight.
With a tear in my eye I see the last of the light fade away,
I have a bad feeling this darkness is here 2 stay.
Everything in my life is now lives in total pitch black,
I find myself on my knees praying 2 hear the voice of the morning lark.
I can no longer contain these feeling of dark night,
Praying that morning lark will bring with it the light.
I am now so sad & grow weaker with every
passing second that I am awake,
Realizing there is nothing I can do 2 stop this
demon game from putting my life at stake.

PAPER FRIEND

I can't tell anyone what's happening 2 me,
This is something a normal person could never see.
I can't tell anyone about the feelings I feel,
In case they go 2 other people & on me squeal.
I can't tell anyone about the demons that r destroying my head,
I no what there reactions would be & if they told
anyone else I would be better of dead.
I can't tell anybody about my anger my depression
my loneliness my addiction my fear,
They would only think the worst & if it got out it would cost me dear.
From the real world I hide behind a happily disguised lee,
I don't have anyone 2 talk 2 no 2 listen 2 me.
A empty tear hits every page that I now write,
With no 1 by my side when I speak I only hear my
Owen tear filled echo in the lonely night.
My paper is now the only thing I confined in it's
the only thing that truly no's who I am,
It also no's the person writing on it is no longer a normal man.
But I have to get this out of my system somehow someway,
So I put pen 2 paper & write how I feel on that night or day.
When I am alone with my paper I can release the stress valves I can pour
on2 paper all these emotional demons that r trying 2 take my very life,
Before I discovered writing I had no way of
releasing all this built up dark evil strife.
For the time being my paper friend is the only thing helping me cope,
But the demons r getting 2 strong & around my neck
the game is beginning 2 tighten the rope.
You see my paper friend can only absorb my emotions it can't talk back,
This is something my paper friend does sadly lack.

I don't know how much longer the strength of
my paper friend can help me stand,
Without someone 2 talk 2 someone 2 give me
guidance I cannot come back in2 safely land.
Sadly my paper friend does not possess the power
2 make me once again a normal man,
But my paper friend is giving me as much strength as it possibly can.
At least I know my paper friend will be here anytime I need to write,
& the way things r going he'll be very busy day & night.
My paper friend is allowing me 2 record everything
about my life in the demon games hell,
& he'll keep 2 himself & only if I live 2 the
world my story will I be able 2 tell.

PAIN

Yet again I sit on another Sunday feeling all alone,
My heart with no beat cold like stone.
I feel my soul is out in the distance were it won't allow me 2 see,
It no's i have fucked up again lying hear totally out my tree.
There is only 1 way for people like me,
Only 1 way to set these demons free.
People only see the lee I want 2 show the act they can't see inside
me they can't see the destruction & overwhelming pain,
I am not strong enough for this the game &
its demons r driving me insane.
I can hear the demons loud in my head,
Yet nothing from my heart quiet & so painfully dead.
The pain everyday seems 2 double,
The demons r 2 strong and my life's in real trouble.
Inside I am so weak & impure,
Just a scared little boy desperately needing a miracle cure.
Scared 2 tell the world he's in pain,
In case the world isn't ready yet & just brands him insane.
Scared 2 tell the world how the demon game really makes him feel,
In case the worlds not ready yet & makes him ask for
forgiveness wile before them he must beg & Neal.
Scared 2 ask the world for help with his fears,
Begging the world 2 stop his pain 2 stem his tears.
This scared little boy doesn't know which way
2 turn which direction 2 take,
In case the demons have a hand in it & it
leads him 2 his last & fatal mistake.
I can no longer see a way through I can no longer
see a end 2 this overwhelming dark pain,
I have just tried 2 explain but u will not understand &
my explanation has once again been in vain.
I can see the demons there on their way,
Don't know how much longer in this place I have the strength 2 stay.

COMING DOWN

Slowly my control is coming back & i am starting 2 take in
my surroundings' making some sense of the conversations
this must mean the buzz has passed its peak,
The demons will strike now when they no
am so very fragile & so very week.
There is 2 much trying 2 go through my head at once I can't process
all the emotions & thoughts that r exploding through my veins,
All that's processed is get away from these emotions &
thoughts before they turn 2 feelings of pain.
I am coming down fast but all I want is 2 go back
up & once again be totally out my face,
Some people can cope with the comedown I
can't & yes I no it's a fucking disgrace.
My head is so fucked up by the demons of drugs when I start to
comedown there is a total breakdown in mental & emotional
strength they seuss 2 function leaving me unable 2 cope,
Without the promise of more drugs or drink I think of
giving in because I can't find anything 2 give me hope.
I just can't find anything 2 combat the way coming down makes me feel,
The demons also no when am coming down before them I will kneel.
This is what the demons have made of me someone
who is afraid of what is in his Owen head,
They've overwhelmed every piece of me that gave me strength
knowing that without strength I am as good as dead.
The demons no when am coming down my heart & soul r lost,
They also no I'll do anything they say no matter
the physical emotional or mental cost.
They no that even in the small time I spend in the real world I am week,
& when am coming down there strength hits its peak.
I guess this is what 2 me coming down means,
But when am coming down nothing is quite what it seems.

BROKEN BODY

My body is a shell of its former self all that's left is a total wreck,
No sign of life up or down from the neck.
My skin is ruff old dry & flaking in places,
Looking at pictures from the past its like looking at 2 different faces.
Bags that r ever present under my eyes,
So run down with every new week come more sty's.
My insides that r constantly in pain,
I fear something is going to brake under this constant relentless strain.
I can't remember the last time my piss was clear
always dark brown with a little hint of red,
Is this my insides telling me that without serous help their dead.
My noise bleeds leave little blotches like petals that fall from a red willow,
Every morning little petals litter my pillows.
When I don't put drugs in2 my system my body
goes in2 a total state of physical pain,
No longer r the comedowns just in my head no
longer do they just drive me insane.
I have took so much out of my body & not once
did I think to put anything back,
I have destroyed my body by staying in the demon
games self destructive drug addictive track.
Blood on my pillows & traces of blood all throughout my piss,
If the demons of the game don't get me my body will
because the destruction you simply cannot miss.

NOBODY

From the first breath we take on that first day we arrive,
All the world seems 2 do is slap Our asses & tell us man up survive.
We all come in2 this world so innocent & pure,
Yet all the world gives us is the promise of insecure.
Why is there never nobody there 2 tell U what in your life is in store,
2 tell U 2 skip the bad live the good stay away
from the state of mental bore.
Nobody realizes the ineffability is at some point every1 needs
help with their life B4 it fades from the worlds sight,
Yet there is never an ineffable NOBOBY 2 tell u when u
need 2 here the words everything is going 2 B alright.
Why is there NOBODY there 2 pick U up when
everything in life is putting U down,
Why won't they pick U up why is that NOBODY ever around.
Is there NOBODY ever around because U
yourself don't want NOBODY there,
Is there never a NOBODY there because the world simply no longer cares.
Is there NOBODY there because U feels as if U R
living within the pages of a fairytale book,
Or is there NOBODY there because U R the only 1 who
can translate it & the world is scared 2 look.
So is there NOBODY there because your life scares them all away,
Is this why U feel NOBODY ever wants 2 stay.
Why is there NOBODY around 4 the less fortunate of this world why
R we looked ap on as if we have been cursed by some evil witch,
Yet why is there so many NOBODYS around
if U R a bitch a dick famous or rich.

DARK CLOUDS

I awake 2 another dark morning lately it's always the same,
How much longer can I keep up playing this
soul destroying killer demon game.
The clouds r dark & grey no blue light in sight,
My life has become stuck in the demon games deadly night.
Life is now so distant so obscured so lonely so grey,
Will the sunshine ever return 2 show me that beautiful warm loving day.
Why does my heart hurt so bad why is it broken in two,
& why do I know it will never heal like new.
The easy way for me would b 2 give up die & leave,
But if I do this friends & family would only b left 2 grieve.
Yet for me & my pain please stop it all,
After all in evolution my life is so petty meaningless & small.
The days r dark always like night,
Please god helps me rediscover my life's light.
I don't care if it hurts I want back my control,
Perfect body mind & forgiveness from my soul.
Yet the dark clouds r up above the darkness is
setting in its all black no sight of light,
This scared little boy feels he has lost his fight.
I now know how it feels 2 be on the way 2 hell,
The emotions r something you could never imagine or begin 2 tell.
The demons now find playing with my head is just a bore,
Because all they here is me screaming please please no more.
They said I was the boy with a thousand expressions a million
jokes with me came laughter smiles i always brought all the joy,
How could someone of that description allow the demons 2
destroy you throw you away like a old disused broken toy.
While I have some sanity left I feel I should say my goodbye's,
This way it's coming from my heart where the demons don't
yet have the influence to make its final beats lie.
I hear the demons there calling me taunting me shouting my name,
Oh my dear beautiful God this really is the end of my demon game.

DO OR DIE

I don't know if there is a end 2 this darkness & pain,
Don't know wither 2 give up or 2 continue 2 fight the demon game.
I have no strength left 2 fight yet somehow I can't seem 2 give in,
Please God deliver me from the demon games overpowering sin.
This is the worst place I could possibly be,
No doors left 2 open so I have no chance of setting myself free.
Trying 2 tell what's left of me that I am still strong,
Catch 22 the demons no I've been in the game far 2 long.
Every time I manage 2 muster a little strength in my head,
2 steps in front r the demons & they crush it dead.
The tiny piece of me that is still alive will somehow continue the fight,
Desperately needing a miracle or its death in the
Demon games lonely dark painful night.
You cannot begin 2 imagine the battles that
right now r raging inside my head,
The only question being will I manage 2 stay
alive or am I as good as dead.

TWO LIVES'S

It's crazy what you think about at your lowest point all
the memories that flood through your head,
Memories you haven't thought about for so
long you were sure they were dead.
Before my mum and dad split up I stayed on a
paradise island four hundred miles away,
Now I reside in Ardrossan Ayrshire the shit hole I was dumped in to stay.
From my first life I can remember all the amazing
times I had its just a pity there all in the past,
Knowing that things would be oh so different if
my first life had been destined to last.
I can clearly remember as a boy I used to build the best go carts in town,
It's quite ironic how most of this second life I have spent
dismantling tearing & bringing myself down.
I can clearly remember my father taking me
fishing & shooting in the hills,
It's quite ironic how most of this second life I only have
distorted memories of snorting thousands of cocaine filled
lines swallowing thousands of killer ecstasy pills.
The jump of life's was something I didn't
want but it was out off my control,
The sinner who caused the jump lied & in doing
that condemned my life to this hell hole.
In my first life I was always happy there was always
a heartwarming smile on my face,
Now there is nothing but a frown because this second life has
been nothing short of a self inflicted drug abusing disgrace.
I'll always wonder that if I was still in my first life what
now would I be doing were now would I be,
This answer I will never know but the life I lead now would
have been something I would never have thought to see.
This second life fuels my DEMON HALF as he brings me
another step closer to my death he will not let me live,
I keep praying & hoping that this second life
has something good yet to give.

MEMORIES

Memories r amazing crazy weird small but complicated things,
Some r easily remembered some take a bit of prompting
before with a little bell the memory rings.
You have your good amazing memories the type that can give
your heart a warm tingling glow whenever u think of one,
Good memories r the easiest to remember because they are stored
in your mind & heart along with the other privileged some.
As much as we don't want them we all still have our
bad memories that you wish u could forget delete from
your mind the one's that broke your heart,
Every time 1 pops into your head dark depressing
emotions come with them right from the start.
Then you get the uncertain memories the 1'ns you r not sure if they r
true or just something in your mind left to wonder around your head,
Like when you see someone & think to yourself i was told he was dead.
Then comes the crazy memories where half of them will
have you laughing so hard your sides become so sore,
the other half though can leave you scared saying
stop these memories I can't take no more.
Then come the foggy memories which i feel i have had
far too many of also known as the vague kind,
Partial blackouts through drugs & drink r to blame for
those distorted memories for my distorted mind.
Thousands of ecstasy tablets have robbed me of massive pieces
of my short term memory this is the bit I hate the most,
Even today my short term memory doesn't function & those
massive missing pieces r as clear to see as an invisible ghost.

Memories I cherish the most are from my long term memory like the
1 of me standing in the hills above cunnings burgh looking down
on punsta place when I was just a child at the tender age of 5,
These memories remember me that there was a time when
i was 100% pure when i was not corrupted by drugs a
time when i understood the feelings of being alive.
Now more than ever my battered bruised broken heart needs these
memories to fall back on to be able to remember it's self that not
all my life has been drug afflicted stuck in this dark pause,
These memories are solid proof that tell my heart i must
keep going keep fighting there is still some just cause.

MY PRAYER

God I am now so weak I only have a few things
left to ask will the pain ever stop,
You now I'm running out of time on the demon games killer clock.
Now more than ever I realize what my old life meant to me,
Why can't the game & its demons go away why can't this they see.
Looking back over everything I have lost,
God do you think I will ever get a chance 2 repay some of the cost.
God the demons r telling me 2 stop fighting let my life go,
But my broken heart still has enough power for
the time being 2 tell the demons no.
God I hate myself for falling so easily in2 the demon games trap,
It was like falling asleep and in2 hell as I awoke from my nap.
God without my soul I can't stop the demons driving me insane,
Please help me find it so I can put a stop 2 this overwhelming pain.
God everyone keep saying time is the only
healer this is what they all seem 2 say,
They don't have 2 live with the killer demons every
second of every minute of every day.
God I no longer feel I only see everyday life at a far of fleeting glance,
Please take me out of the demon game or at
least give me a fighting chance.

WAITING

Only a few question now run through my head
& 1 is do you think god herd me pray,
Can he find it in his heart 2 forgive me let me
come back 2 his side back 2 his way.
Or has being so long in the demon game filled
my life with so much self-inflicted sin,
That God feels the only place for me is with
the devil & his demons in hells bin.
Do you think God will judge me on what
throughout the demon game I have done,
Do you think he will judge me on what the
demons have made me become.
Am I worthy of his time does he deem my life
worthy enough to give it a thought,
What will he think when he looks over and sea's the demons of the
game have crushed my heart & soul they so easily destroyed the lot.
In me will he only see the overwhelming self-destruction
& say the demons in me should not be unlocked,
Or will he see me for what I truly am a stupid scared
little boy that has strayed 2 far from his flock.
Will he be able 2 understand the reasons
behind my broken heart & lost soul,
Will he find enough good left in me 2 give me his help 2 piece
my life back together try & make it once again whole.
All I know is that every second 2 the demon game
I lose more of this already lost fight,
I only hope that I will be given the chance 2 again feel & see life's light.

GOODBYE

I have been waiting but I don't think God herd me pray &
now my time has run out with only a few things left 2 say,
To all the people I love please don't blame your self's because I choose
2 leave you on this cold Decembers night live with the knowledge
there was nothing you could have said or done 2 make me stay.
Please try 2 understand that I could no longer live within the demon
games hell where everything in my life is nothing but lies & disgrace,
Please don't cry over me for I will b on my way 2 a much better place.
My conscious tells me I made my bed & now on it I must lie,
My head tells me this is where my overwhelming
pain stops this bed is my place die.
My broken body tells me it has been pushed
2 far it has nothing left 2 give,
Only heaven can fix my broken body here
on earth its now 2 painful 2 live.
I can no longer face living in this empty shell of the old me,
I am willing 2 make the ultimate sacrifice 2 have
a chance of getting back the old lee.
I hope god will forgive me for my sins & will be
waiting for me to sit me by his side,
Then my soul will rest in peace floating along with
the angels on one of heavens beautiful tides.
So to all the people I love please don't be sad
for 1 day we will once again meat,
When it's your turn to come through the gates
hopefully you will see me sitting at gods feet.
GOODBYE GOODBYE GOODBYE

THE VOICE OF GOD

This may sound crazy but tonight I spoke
with god to me he really did speak,
With a relaxed soothing voice he answered every
question I threw at him he told me it wasn't 2 late for
me 2 turn my life around to get back on my feet.
He told me that in my life certain changes were going
2 bring back some much needed warmth & sun,
He told me I was 2 hang on dig in my life
changing chance was about 2 come.
He told me that certain things in my future would change
these certain things he thought I should no,
He told me of these changes because he knew that they
would give me the hope I needed 2 give life 1 more go.
He told me that I was going to get some of the things that
for so long my life had been in such desperate need,
He told me it was time 2 destroy the demons 2 destroy their very seed.
He told me he was sending a guardian angel 2 help show me the way,
He told me in the demon games hell I was no longer destined 2 stay.
He told me he was willing to save my soul & in return
I was 2 finish writing the demon game,
He told me to open my eyes & see that from this point if i was
willing 2 take the chance life would never be the same.

LIFE OR DEATH

My body & head still favor death they tell me they have
nothing left 2 give they tell me 2 take the easy way out,
My heart & soul once again favor life they say we may have a shout.
No matter what it is I can never seem 2 pick answers that r all the same,
This is just another evil twist 2 the irony of THE DEMON GAME.
On 1 hand the demons had won & I was ready to die,
On the other hand God now tells me there is
hope all I have 2 do is give it 1 more try.
If I go with the demons this is where it will end no longer will I
b always left with the feelings & thoughts of going insane,
I will b able 2 rest in peace for me there will be no more pain.
If I go with God I will have 2 continue 2 go
through this overwhelming dark strife,
Is it really worth it for another chance at an already fucked up life.
But there is something from the depths of my broken
heart telling me I must give this life one more go,
Its telling me I must find out if what God told me is true
my conscious says these things my soul must no.
I must have a go at this last chance that is here for me 2 take,
Looks like its going 2 b a little longer before anyone has
to turn up to my funeral & sit through my wake.
I have already pushed my body mind heart & soul whey beyond their
limits I have took out of them more than they were ever designed 2 give,
Let's see how much more I can push them so
I may take this chance & live.

DARKEST MILE

I am still not 100% sure if I am going 2 make it
through what is my life's darkest mile,
What chance have I got when my life still hasn't
got what it needs 2 make me smile.
The alarm bells won't stop ringing as reality begins to set,
Seems am still trapped here by the demon
games all powerful unbreakable net.
They say when you hit rock bottom up is the only way,
So why do I seem 2 b in this place for an everlasting stay.
Today I began 2 experience a feeling I cannot
explain all I know is I have never felt it be4,
don't know if it's a bad thing or if I should be wanting more.
Over the past few weeks this feeling has begun 2 increase,
It's the only thing stopping the demons dragging
my soul 2 the graveyard of the desist.
It's the first thing that has been strong enough 2 stand by
my side even in the demon games long deadly night,
This feeling is now beginning to drag me along somehow
its has started to help me with the fight.
In my life there is definitely something beginning
to change am not sure what or how,
But what ever this feeling is its giving me the
strength to fight of the demon game for now.
Maybe through the darkness there was something
the demons did not want me 2 see,
I know the demons r scared of this feeling that
is trying to pull me out set me free.
Maybe the darkness its self has decided to show
mercy & give me back a life of relative plain,
Or maybe GOD as promised has sent me a guardian angel
to show me the way out of THE DEMON GAME.

TALKING PAPER

When I first started writing it was just away for me to clear
my head of all the built up dark overpowering strife,
In the beginning my writing was the only thing that
stopped me losing control of my shattered broken life.
But now I realize that what I have been writing is the
beginnings of a book 2 & 2 me this is now so clear to see,
For the first time my paper is talking shouting screaming back at me.
My paper is saying write record describe then tell it to all,
This is turning into something hugh yet it started
life as that 1 little poem so dark so small.
Now when I write I no longer have to think its
just there spilling out of my head,
Its as if I already know what am about 2 write its
clearer than something I have just said.
I think god has just helped save my soul so that
the demon game would b my story to tell,
God is telling me to keep writing 2 explain 2 the world everything
about the demon games overpowering drug afflicted living hell.
For the first time I don't feel scared 2 open the
pages & tell the world of the demon game,
I now know there is people who will understand I know there
is millions out there going through something the same.

GODS ANGEL

On that lonely cold Decembers night when I prayed to
GOD asking for his help with my everlasting fight,
I don't know how but I new he was listening I
new he would answer my cry's of plight.
He has sent me 1 of his angels to try & turn my darkness back in2 light,
Here to try & get me out of the demon games painfully addictive night.
His angel is helping to drive the dark clouds
away in2 the distance out of sight,
I can now look up & see tiny pieces of blue sky its been so
long that to me they're pieces of heavens very light.
I know his angel is here 2 see me through these crazy times night & day,
My storm is passing over the dark clouds r most
certainly being driven all b it slowly away.
I awoke this morning & on my face was a smile,
I hadn't done that for such a long long wile.
God you have just saved my life somehow you've
stopped me from going insane,
I am eternally grateful 2 you for trying 2 put
a stop 2 my overwhelming pain.
What I did 2 deserve such an angel I will never know always wonder,
An angel so powerful its silencing even the demons thunder.

CRAZY

You may think that I am crazy you may say that I
am you may think I have lost the plot,
But the plot is the demons of drugs r crazy & me well am not.
In order for you to totally understand how I fell you would have
had 2 have gone or be going through something like what I am
then with my situation you would b able 2 fully get 2 grips,
I hope you will never b stupid enough to put your self through anything
like this because of your life it tears massive irreplaceable strips.
Yes you learn 2 cope with the game you learn 2 control
the demons that were trying 2 take your very life,
But the mental & emotional scares you will always have
as if the demons used on you a razor sharp knife.
At this moment in my life is it crazy for me 2 try & work out who
I am am I scum for what the demons have made me become,
Or am I special for controlling the demons &
leading my life back out in2 a little sun.
Am I crazy for wishing the destruction will sort its self out,
Am I crazy for thinking if I wish hard enough
I may just b in with a shout.
Am I crazy for thinking that inside my head &
heart I can keep all this dark strife,
Am I crazy for believing I can rebuild my life.
Is it crazy for me 2 now look ahead with a little hope in my heart,
Is it crazy for me 2 say I am confident I can make a fresh start.
Is it crazy for me 2 think you r reading this & 2
you're self all you can do is frown tot and sie,
Is it so crazy for me 2 think that you now see through
THE DEMON GAME & realize all I want 2 do is
go back 2 being an average everyday guy.

Is it so crazy that now you can see the only
difference between me & you is our pasts,
Is it so crazy to know that in my future my
past has no place it will never last.
Am I crazy for now worrying what do people really think of me,
Am I crazy for saying stick with me & you will see the rebirth of lee.
Is it so crazy that at this moment in time I don't
care if you think I am crazy or not,
Is it so crazy to say I think you should read to the end
before you judge me before you call your shot.

MY SECOND BEGINNING

All these years fighting the deadly demon game,
Now trying to repair its destruction different
circumstances but feels just the same.
I just want to see a normal life I pray that I will see that sight,
Finally trying to put all the self inflicted painful wrongs right.
Now on the recovery side of the demon game but
still having to fight as hard as before,
I didn't know my second beginning was going to be
so tough have I enough strength left in store.
Back then if I new my second beginning would be so hard would
I have taken so much out of my heart and soul to win,
All I did realize was I could stop the pain by giving in.
At the time all I wanted was 1 more chance
at life I just wanted 1 more go,
If I had known the work involved would I have been so
quick to take Gods chance this I really don't know.
If I new it was going to be this hard would I have been so
eager to swap demons & darkness for angels and light,
Would I have prayed so hard to GOD to save my
soul on that cold Decembers night.
I wasn't able to foresee how my second beginning would be,
Never did I think will it be happy sad good or bad.
Do I have enough mental strength left to see
this second beginning to its last mile,
To see me stand tall & proud with on my face a heart warming smile.
Once again I find myself asking the question will I make it by,
Or in this second beginning is there one last demon
who's only objective is to see me die.
I know the demons will be watching me
waiting for me to make a mistake,
They know even just one little slip & my soul
will once again be there's to take.

They will wait to see if again I become week so
they can come at me again & again,
They know that even my second beginning will
have its fair share of grief & pain.
I do know one thing it was the powers above that got me to
were I am they stepped in when I was as good as dead,
So at least I know in getting here I have not been mislead.
Even if I am not strong enough to see out my second
beginning if on this path it is were I must die,
At least on my way through heavens gates I can turn
to GOD & with pride say I gave it my best try.

REALITY

I thought I had nothing left 2 fight my overwhelming affliction,
I know I have destroyed my self over my addictions.
I am scared that all the damage 2 my head heart & body
is irreversible i know its already been well over done,
Will I be able 2 function normally or am I dammed
like a blind man looking for the sun.
I am scared its taken me 2 long 2 rediscover my faith 2 turn & fight,
Even if I am strong enough i now realize everything
will never go back to100% right.
This second beginning is some price 2 pay,
All I did was try 2 live my life the rock stars way.
Inside me I still mostly feel lonely & cold,
Why didn't this stupid little boy listen 2 the
warnings that at the beginning he was told.
I feel as if I was already out of time before I was told,
I now have 2 live the rest of my life with the knowledge
that I will never get back the lee of old.
The overpowering reality of THE DEMON
GAME is now beginning 2 set in,
The last nineteen years I have been living in total self sin.
But I must keep my head up & hopefully day by day I will get stronger,
& with a little help maybe my heart will once
again smile & the pain will b no longer.
Now for what is left of me I must try 2 make up for
some of what I have lost for what I have done,
Maybe that blind mans not so blind & he's screaming he can see the sun.

STRENGTH

As I sit here looking up at the stars I forgot how beautiful life could be,
All these years fighting THE DEMON GAME
made me blind 2 what I could not see.
Although I was smiling on the outside inside I
could only muster a sad lonely frown,
All the years fighting the demons took so much
out of me they always kept me down.
My conscious tells me I am responsible I am the only 1 to blame,
My heart tells me it was the demons that put out destroyed my flame.
Looking back at what THE DEMON GAME has done 2 my
life knowing how much irreversible destruction it's done,
But looking forward & seeing through these troubled
times stronger I am now beginning 2 become.
Now finally I am starting 2 turn things around
starting 2 put the wrongs right,
What a feeling 2 now your life is back in some all be it just a little light.
The road I have just come down was evil dark lonely & so very long,
Rediscovering my faith in GOD & life were the defining
moments that gave me the hope I needed 2 become strong.
So God I promise you I am going 2 do all I can,
To keep becoming a stronger wiser better man.

HALFWAY

I don't know how but I have managed to stay alive through
the dark side of THE DEMON GAME & found in me
strength I thought I would never rediscover,
So now I must stay strong my head heart body
& soul all need time to recover.
I must make sure there r no demons trying to hide out of site,
Give them half a chance & they will get me with there second bite.
But this time I know the demon games number one trap,
I won't be caught for a second time on the nap.
Now I am taking one day at a time there's no
point in planning to far ahead,
Still to week if I get it wrong there's a chance
I could still have to face death.
I can only look forward & hope my recovery comes quick & fast,
I have made it half way so I don't want to slow down be left running last.

SMALL THINGS

In life we all come face 2 face with overwhelming grief & pain,
So who am I 2 moan grumble or complain.
My existence has made me realize that in life it's the small
things that count make it happen always make you smile,
Small things will always be a guiding light even in your darkest mile.
It's the small things that give you that amazing feeling
a natural high you can never quite explain,
They make you glow so happy that for a wile
even the darkest of life's have no pain.
Without your small things you would be stuck
in a life of dark lonely night,
You need your small things 2 keep in front of you the light.
Your small things make life worth wile give you all the
reasons 2 keep going all the reasons 2 live,
Your small things will help show you the way in life
this is 1 of the many things 2 you they give.
My small things are God,BIG chief slim,Gman,BIG bro,Mum friends
& close family simply because of the way they always make me feel,
To my small things I happily give praise in
front of them I would happily kneel.
So never mind money or fame,
Cherish the small things keep your life happy & plain.
Keep your small things close 2 your heart
were they cannot be taken away,
Because in your darkest hour it will b one of your small things
that will make you realize in life is were you must stay.

THE BATTLE OF SIDES

My 2 halves r still fighting a deadly battle
which has left them side by side,
But this time the good in me is winning I can feel myself
being pulled out of the deadly dark drowning tide.
The strength i am using is coming from deep within my
broken heart & i fear its putting on it 2 heavy a toll,
I fear i am using more than it can give 2 stop the
demons being able 2 regain control.
Only when my heart & mind r working as one,
Am I confident the games demons will never take back my life's sun.
Its impossible for me 2 destroy my dark side
its impossible for me 2 kill it dead,
But my good side has caged it in locked it away
deep inside the fortress that is my head.
You see my dark side draws its strength from the
addiction sections within your all powerful brain,
It uses my brains many resources 2 engulf overwhelm self preserve & gain.
When my dark sides demons were in control
all they wanted 2 do was destroy,
They abused & used my body as there transport
like batteries inside a robot toy.
The only catch is your dark side is constantly being fed from
the brain so its strength will never fade or become week,
So for your good side 2 stay 1 step in front it must
become sneaky intelligent & sleek.
So remember no matter how strong your dark
side is 2 beat it there is always a way,
Just learn 2 master your emotional controls &
your good side can stay out & safely play.

SPIKED

I can't believe this I have been spiked & I am totally out of my face,
I had 2 leave the pub in a hurry I couldn't
stay 1 more minute in that place.
I have now got back 2 my flat & still I cannot
believe what has just happened 2 me,
I have fought so hard 2 get away from these feelings
that come with being totally out your tree.
All of a sudden its like being put back 2 square one,
Scared the demons will once again steel my life's sun.
But slowly I start 2 realize this buzz isn't like what it used 2 be,
For I still feel strong inside & the sun I can clearly see.
For the first time I don't feel the overwhelming need for more,
For the first time I am settling my Owen emotional & mental score.
Totally in control of the demons that r once
again running throughout my head,
I won't allow the demons 2 once again let me be mislead.
Totally in control of this buzz that I am getting from what i think is a e,
No longer do I need 2 feed an addiction no longer do I
feel the constant need 2 be totally out my tree.
It just goes 2 show how strong I have become there's
now way I will be dragged back down,
So much am I in control I now realize I could
have easily stayed out on the town.
So I am just going 2 sit back & enjoy the rest of my night,
For the first time in years I won't be scared 2 open
the blinds & welcome the mornings light.
For I no longer fear the end of the buzz I no
longer fear coming back 2 reality,
I know I can face these things because its
something I now have in my mentality.

RECOVERING HEAD

I still wait for the demons I have beat 2 speak,
As if I had just put them down & now they will rise
2 once again reach their overwhelming peak.
But I have concord my demons they r as good as dead,
Suppose it's just a scared feeling from my
dysfunctional but recovering head.
This is probably natural from being so long in the
overpowering dark destructive demon game,
Am not used 2 this normal life so easy straight forward basic & plain.
It is hard trying 2 readjust trying 2 find my feet in this normal life,
Am 2 used to playing THE DEMON GAME hanging my
life by a thread over the edge of a razor sharp knives.
Don't get me wrong my new life is what I want this is my number 1 need,
It just seems that a part of me still needs my
old life so it may continue 2 feed.
I am staring 2 grow in 2 this new life my newborn self has given,
Now I rely on the buzz of life 2 give me strength 2 keep me driven.
So with this new life let's see how far I can
take it lets see how high I can go,
I have no excuses now there is nothing 2 keep me down heavy or slow.
To get this new life this second chance my head heart body and
soul fought an internal war they have no right to be winning my
additive side took from them things that can never be replaced but
bruised battered & broken they r wining & r giving me something
I have not had for years a chance to face life from a even plain,
Personally I don't think I deserve a second chance when it
was the other half of me that destroyed my Owen heart, body,
mind & soul but be that as it may I will grab this one by the
horns even with the knowledge that it won't b the same.

MAGIC EMOTIONS

Why is the magic so potent its spells of emotions take the weakest
2 the stars bring the strongest 2 there knees bad go good good go
blind all because of the chemicals exploding through your mind,
What is it that allows us 2 feel such a wide rage of
emotions from cruel despair 2 ecstatic & kind.
Why R we aloud 2 feel so many different emotions,
Why do we use our body's 2 interpret these potent spells
coursing through our vanes in massive explosions.
Why is it when in love U R always the last 2 know
what is it about that spell that makes U blind,
Why can't U control who U fall in love with why can't
U control the magic that lies within your mind.
Why when heartbroken do the spells turn 2 black magic bringing the
walls of your emotional life crashing down leaving only the wish 2 die,
& why can we never admit 2 being heartbroken about
this 1 peace of black magic we always lie.
What is that could put so much potency in2 the spells
that cause overwhelming loneliness & pain,
Why isn't there an instant potion we can take
2 counter act it b4 it drives us insane.
Why does hour owen magic allow us 2 feel such pain
that it can drive a person 2 take there owen life,
Why R we dammed 2 b able 2 feel such potent painful dark strife.
Why is it that no matter how many people U have around
you the magic makes U feel like U R all alone,
What is it in this big bad world that consistently
makes U feel emotionally on your owen.
Why R U aloud 2 get so excited about even the
smallest of your life's trivial things,
Why R those spells so potent U feel U can fly without wings.

What kind of magic is it that allows us 2 feel hope in
times of our life's when we thought there was none,
The spell of hope that puts U back on the steps of happiness
instantly a better person U once again become.
Imagine what life would B like if U never found your door to
unlock all these magical emotions that R the basis of your
existence without them U would b as good as the living dead,
If we were incapable of feeling emotion life would B empty
emptiness would B the only thing filling our heart & heads.
So now like me U must realize that all these emotions
like love heart ache pain loneliness excitement hope
depression R all but 1 potent magical emotion,
U realize that U get all these different feelings from 1 by the way
U take back the overpowering overwhelming potent explosions.

DEMON

There is 1 demon though which I can't destroy
can't shake can't seem 2 get it 2 go away,
This demon is ever present there with me every minute of every day.
This demon is much stronger than any other there has ever been,
It's so strong that inside me from time 2 time
the demon I see & have always seen.
The game gave birth 2 this demon with the sole purpose
2 haunt me right up 2 the day that I die,
I know exactly what this demon is because 2 myself I no longer lie.
It's just something I have learn to live with something I try to control,
But if the demon gets out on2 my heart it puts a heavy toll.
I hear you asking why I can't destroy this demon
why does it always sit by my side,
This demon always stays close 2 me just like
the way a fish follows the tide.
You see to destroy this demon first I would have 2 destroy me,
And 2 do such acts 2 myself is something I can no longer see.
There is much more 2 this demon than first meets the eye,
It's something I have learn t 2 leave alone its better of being left 2 lie.
So I can't destroy the demon this part is so straight
forward that even a blind man would be able to see,
I'll let you in2 a little secret I can't destroy the demon
because the demon is the other half of me.

THE BIGGER GAME

It dives into your deepest thoughts & brings them
to the surface so you can be easily mislead,
Anyone who has been unfortunate enough to have played against the
demon game no's it first gets to you as tiny thoughts in your head.
It then dives straight into gain control over
your deepest darkest emotions,
It then controls you by sending them back in
uncontrollable massive dark explosions.
It then goes for the killer blow & dives into your
most terrifying deepest darkest fears,
It knows it has absolute power over you if it can control your tears.
The bigger game is in everything to do with addiction it's
everywhere you look from TV to the papers you read,
Sometimes the bigger game does not stand out until
someone paints a picture for your head.
And with every passing second it gets stronger for as soon as anyone
takes a drug they become a foot soldier for the bigger game,
It tells them to rob steel pick up that knife or gun and aim.
& it has foot soldier's all over the globe every town
has its drug users this is a fact not a lie,
& all it has to do to keep its foot soldiers is
simply keep giving them a high.
There r more drugs they are cheaper easier to
get & it looks like there here to stay,
So no matter where you go you will never get away
from the overwhelming size & strength of the bigger
game there will always be a part of it near bye.

I SEE

I see things that not to many other people have the knowledge to see,
I see through the hidden darkness & watch as the demons take
lost souls to where THE DEMON GAME wants them to be.
I see THE DEMON GAME as it takes more
& more children under its wing,
If only they could see the LIVING hell within
THE DEMON GAMES deadly sting.
I see young minds as they go through the first
stages of THE DEMON GAME,
But they don't want to listen to the advice of an old
wise head that has been through the same.
I see THE DEMON GAME smile as it gets ever closer to its final goal,
Its final goal being to destroy every last drug free soul.
I see THE DEMON GAME as it engulfs everything that is all,
The human races resistance is emotionally week & mentally to small.
I see THE DEMON GAME taking more & more
souls as it sweeps un hindered over the land,
The human race can't see it yet but is nears it
final defeat its final drug free stand.
I see THE DEMON GAME every direction I turn its everywhere I look,
GOD helps save my soul so to you I could put a warning in this book.

DARK CHILDREN

All throughout the years my fight has been with
THE DEMON GAME & its deadly night,
Drug demons so dark they have not yet herd of the word light.
But there is a side to the dark side that not to many people no,
It's a side that not even the darkest demons can or will go.
This is the side that the dark children patrol,
This is the side that the dark children control.
Dark children r simply people who have experienced
both sides of drugs the good & the bad,
They r the ones who accept & take the blame for their Owen
overwhelming emotional self destruction the price they paid
to make it through the demons without going mad.
In a way they r like GODS living angels who can & choose
to work within THE DEMON GAMES emotionally
physically mentally dangerous deadly sides,
They posses the knowledge to be able to stop the demons
dragging lost souls onto the engulfing dark drowning tides.
They r the only ones who will fully understand why you need
someone by your side & never will u need to ask them to stay,
When you r in the demon game they r the only ones with the
first hand knowledge needed to try & help show you the way.
Just think of them as beautiful guiding stars in the night sky,
There to help guide lost souls to were in safety & comfort they may lie.
Never underestimate them always take the time
to listen to what they have to say,
For with your life they will show you how to
keep THE DEMON GAME at bay.
To become one of these dark children you must first
gamble your life against THE DEMON GAME,
999 out of a 1000 gambles fail to make it & the other 1 well as
you've just been reading they will never be 100% the same.
Wither I like it or not 1 of these dark children I have become
the knowledge & experience needed now lies within me,
You never no maybe 1 day I will have the
chance to set a tortured soul free.

EXPLANATIONS

How could I hid it for so long,
How could I hide something that was so very wrong.
How do I explain how I hid THE DEMON GAME for so long,
Well it's like turning on a radio & hearing no song.
I hid it behind a boy they just thought liked to party,
The boy with all the jokes the little pants of smarty.
You see I didn't hang around with the same group of friends for that long,
I would disappear before anyone had a chance to find
out that inside me things were so very wrong.
I would only stay with that certain group until
they no longer wanted to party like hell,
That was my cue to move on before anyone put 2
and 2 together before they were able 2 tell.
I would quickly find another group of friends that were willing
to party this way I had an excuse to always be out my face,
This way no one would ever see that inside me I was
nothing but a heavy drug abusing disgrace.
By constantly moving from group to group of friends no 1
person would ever be able to fully gage the massive amounts
of drugs I was taking they would only see little bits that to
them would look like nothing more than a bit of greed,
Only I knew the total amounts only I knew I was taking through need.
By always partying like hell it gave me a front to hide behind
it done its job & hid just how much drugs I did swallow,
You would have thought that after thousands of pills & powder
I would be full up inside how ironic all it done was add 2
the darkness make me more empty even more hollow.
The demons were very smart & always managed to cover
my tracks hide from these friends the real lee,
They made sure that the real lee was something
they would never get a chance 2 meet 2 see.

All these friends only new me as the lee who
with them loved to get out his face,
They never knew me before the demon game so they would
never have new that party's weren't the real lee's place.
The demons hide me behind a well disguised foolproof constant lie,
They hide me so well that not even I could find any trace of
the real me no matter where I looked or how hard I tried.
So now you no the reasons why in me the demon game
by these friends was never discovered never found,
The demons kept me on the move always there but never around.

MISSING LINK

One thing I have noticed about my life is there is a missing link,
I don't know what it is I am looking for but am
scared I miss it so I try to not even blink.
I don't know what it is all I know is when I do
find it I will no it's my missing link,
Then maybe I will realize why I keep putting so much
thought into it why over it all I have done is think.
I know that if I find my missing link it will give me the best
chance of finding forgiveness from my torched soul,
I know my missing link will bring me happiness fulfillment make
me feel as close as I can to being emotionally human & whole.
I know my missing link is the only chance I have of once & for
all killing of the raging demon that is the other half of me,
If only I knew what I was to look for if only
it was put in front of me to see.
Will I ever get my missing link is it out there for me to find,
Or will my missing link stay only as a happy
thought I have constantly on my mind.
Will I have to live the rest of my life with inside
me this massive dark empty gaping hole,
Without my missing link I will never gain forgiveness from my soul.
I can only hope & pray my missing link is
out trying to finds its way to me,
With warmth & a loving calm it will fill me with happiness
tell me every things going to be ok for lee.
And once again I say my nightly prayer asking the powers
above to help my missing link track me down,
With no missing link am like a king sitting on
his throne with no jewels or crown.

LOOKING BACK

Looking back over these past few years there's just been too
much craziness to try & fully explain 2 try and take in,
Emotionally I am only half the man I used to be yet I still sit here
proud in the knowledge that even at my life's weakest darkest saddest
loneliest broken no hope moment something special inside me stood
up & delivered me from the demon games overpowering sin.
So special that a lost wreckage of a self inflicted
mangled life was what it had stood up to save,
A life so destroyed that the Owner himself saw nothing left worthy
of saving he had already condemned in to the demon games grave.
It just goes to show that even when you've given
up all hope & think everything is lost,
If you look hard enough there is always something special left inside
you that will not give up the cause that will fight with every last
heart beat that will create miracles no matter to its self the cost.
Yes to the demon game I did lose a thousand battles and onto my heart
head & soul they have left scares permanent deep emotional cuts,
But let's look at the overall bigger picture I won the war
& to that there can be no questions no buts.
I know the answer to why I will never be the person I was
before I entered my war with the demon game,
The answer is me I started destroyed fixed & finished a self inflicted war
fought between my two army's inside 1 living me I raged a war were I was
losing on all sides I am the soul reason why I will never be the same.
Yes I know I have to live knowing that everything emotionally I have
lost is my fault but mentally I have taken gained & been given knowledge
strength & wisdom this part of my life certainly stronger it has become,
To keep the scales balanced for everything taken
something in return has been given and knowing this
allows me to easily live with the scares unlike some.

Considering the hell I have just put myself through
I think I have done not too bad,
Yes emotionally I have been weakened but mentally
& physically I have gained in strength & importantly
when I now look back I am no longer sad.
My biggest concern for the future is preventing another outbreak
of war how do I keep apart two army's that live on 1 battle field,
Do I conceder myself to be strong enough to attempt to merge 2 into
1 or is the reality that between them I will just have to put a shield.
If It hadn't been for the demon game I would never have discovered that
special part of me that no matter what the game throw at me it would
not roll over it would not bend it would not allow me to give in and die,
It's made me realize that on the outside I am average but on the
inside I have something truly special a guiding light that will
always shine through the darkness a light that could not would not
and will not be put out no matter how hard my darkness tries.

TAKE TIME

We never take anytime just to stop take a deep
breathe & look around at this beautiful place,
Life nowadays is liven at such a fast frantic pace.
No one takes time to sit back & look at life from the rear seat,
Everyone seems to live life constantly running around on sore feet.
Everyone's 2 preoccupied trying to better than the person next to them
that we as a race tend to overlook the true meanings 4 instance you
wouldn't see a angler setting up on a river he knows has no trout,
If we don't take time to appreciate the meaning life won't
give you a second go nor will it stand still it will be gone in
a second taking with it your only chance of gaining a little
no towards understanding what it's all truly about.
Everyone's allowing there self's to miss on so much natural
beauty that if u look properly comes with a huge a lower,
Were only interested in immaterial things like getting
rich & staying away from being classed as poor.
Everyone's to busy worrying about their future regretting there past,
I say live life 4 the moment or you will miss your
present & trust me it will disappear way to fast.
Before you know it you will be older & stiffer than a 50ft red oak tree,
So before your body & sight start to age take time to go
out & see all the things you've always wanted to see.
Don't let your life flash by don't piss it up against
a wall don't flushed it down the loo,
Before your body begins to get hindered by the ravages of
time get yourself to do all you've ever wanted to do.
Take time to find something to take you away from the hassles of
everyday life even if it only lets you for a few hours really live,
Always take time to give back all & more love to
those special people that to you give.

Take time to sail away on the buzz that is hassle free life,
Take time to make those special moments for your children
brothers sisters mothers fathers husbands & wife's.
Everyone's so wrapped up in there Owen little lives that no one
takes time to enjoy takes time even for a moment to stop,
Not until they realize it's too late & there life's
timing pin has already dropped.
Take time with yourself even if it's only just to sit back & think,
Take as much time as you need until with the
true meaning of life you begin 2 link.

GATHERED THOUGHTS

I truly wish that I could turn around now & tell U that the damage done
2 my body mind heart & soul R repairing but I can't it would B a lie,
Once U cross in2 the realm which is THE DEMON GAME any damage
done is irreversible like a curse it stays with U right up 2 the day U die.
U just learn 2 live inside your crazy head & after a while
U no which directions U can & cannot take,
This is why U must take time 2 gather your thoughts inside your head
there R still 2 many ways 2 slip on2 that untaken fatal mistake.
I guess the destruction 2 your body heart soul & mind R part of
paying the piper 4 the sins U committed in THE DEMON GAME,
But through gathering your thoughts U slowly learn 2 lock the true
craziness deep inside your head so deep U tend 2 forget its very name.
This is why 4 a few months now my life has been at a bit of a
stand still while I gather my thought ready 4 another big push,
Even now I must look from every angle
making sure it's right B4 I let loose.
Nowadays I tend not 2 rush anything every decision is made
with the same process slow steady & always the same,
I made way 2 many painful mistakes by rushing decisions
back in THE KILLER DEMON GAME.
I make sure I take as much time needed 2 gather my thoughts
even now I don't trust my head 2 make my life's important
decisions I can't trust it 2 tell me what's wrong or right,
For I know my mind can still B easily mislead by my DEMON
half who still lives strong within the killer night.
U have 2 understand that even in my new life everything
is fragile it all hangs by a tender thread,
If I don't take the time needed 2 gather my thoughts the thread could
easily brake & U know what would follow that definition dead.

So when gathering my thoughts I take time
2 ponder dissect & slowly think,
I must make sure in the decisions I make there
R no missing or broken links.
So I will continue 2 take as much time as I need 2
gather these all important thoughts that will push me
slowly & steadily towards my biggest goals,
Keep writing family & true friends close find that special
girl & most importantly forgiveness from my soul.

PAYING THE PIPER

There comes a day in everyone's life when it's there
time to start paying the piper my day has come as if he
is standing in front of me asking for some back,
In my future will this be something that my
rewired dysfunctional life will sadly lack.
My short term memory that was bad enough on drugs
has totally gone now that I am ecstasy free,
The only thing stored in my short term memory is that
for the past 19 years my name has been lee.
My dreams that are no longer nightmares but "freakly"
when I am asleep that's the way they feel,
It's like there is a orange in front of me to eat but I cannot
because I have no knowledge of being able to peal.
I know that because of the countless thousands of drugs I have took
there's a good chance in my future something might go boom,
This is something that will always hang over my
head that around my life it will always loom.
Will the piper let me reach an old age does
my broken body have it to deliver,
The unseen damage I have done to my insides to
my head heart kidneys lungs & liver.
Constantly waiting & praying for forgiveness
from my broken heart & lost soul,
Will the piper allow me to get the things I need
to once again feel human & whole.
I can only live in hope that I am one of the lucky ones
& these things to me might never become,
Or is the piper saying I should be very scared
of my unknown future to come.

But it was me & only me, who created & put myself through the
overwhelming dark punishment that is THE DEMON GAME,
Punishment so destructive that the devil himself tells me
he still has for it no description no title no name.
I always have & always will take full responsibility for what
to myself I have done I must take the sol blame,
Even away back at the start I was smart enough 2 no that even
after taking just one drug I would never be the same.
So I now have to start paying the piper in front
of him I must stand strong & tall,
I only hope he doesn't ask for more than I can give
I can only hope he doesn't ask for all.

I HOPE

I hope that in reading the demon game you have
found something you could relate to,
Maybe a piece you read realizing at one point that was or still is you.
I also hope you did not relate to all that I just did tell,
Knowing that if you did your in a world of self inflicted hell.
Take a good look at yourself in case you've just been the last to
realize your already upgraded from drug taker to demon game
player So just take a little second put everything else on pause,
If you miss the warnings then it will be to late when you realize the
overwhelming destruction playing the demon game will cause.
I hope you can take a little new knowledge from reading the demon
game I hope it will give you a view that before you never had,
I also hope you're not just sitting thinking this boys
lost the plot he has simply gone mad.
I hope you now realize that it's taking drugs that destroy the person
it's their demons that take away the existence of who they are,
& anyone brave enough to get themselves away from THE DEMON
GAME should class themselves there Owen little superstar.
I hope in the writing of THE DEMON GAME there
r some answers for all the other players,
I hope they have found the answers they were looking
for all throughout the demon games layers.
I hope in the writing of THE DEMON GAME you have found
your explanations to why certain people go so far of the rails,
Be fair try not to be too hard because now you know
why everything they seem to do fails.
& if you have never taken a drug I hope THE DEMON
GAME has shown you that's the way it should stay,
& never be so cocky to think THE DEMON
GAME is something you could easily play.

I hope you now fully realize truly how much out of
life's THE DEMON GAME can & will take,
I also truly hope you have read deep into my
1 huge life destroying mistake.
It's too late for me my damage is irreversible its already been done,
It might not be too late for you act now before
the demons r allowed to steal your sun.
And lastly I hope you find yourself before with
the demon game you make a date,
I pray to everything that is all & mighty you
find yourself before its too late.

CREATIVE HEAD

My creative head is getting stronger & becoming
more of an influence in my life,
My thoughts r so sharp it's like they hinge on
the edge of a razor sharp knife.
The world & everything in it is much clearer now that
I look at everything through creative eyes,
Doesn't matter what it is how important or what size.
Everything I now look at is taken in dissected turned
upside down & then processed for what it truly is,
I have missed so much up until now my creative head really is the biz.
There r many pieces to the package that is my creative head
not only can it write it has a unique ability to translate,
No matter how crazy the situation it will translate it
into such simple words that the age group to understand
it would range from 100 to as young as 8.
To most of the population emotions r unexplainable they
can never find the words needed to describe how they
feel it's simply something they cannot explain,
Put any emotion through my creative head & it will translate it
into a universally understood language easily read basic & plain.
Without me even knowing it my creative has took 21 years
of pure insanity & translated it into such simple dialog that
even a dyslexic person could easily read my book,
It has translated the unexplainable into a easily understood language so if
you ever do read THE DEMON GAME you will only have to take 1 look.
With my creative head I am a much more deeper wiser happier man,
My head exploding with creativity my body beneath it in a state of calm.
And the ironic thing is it was THE DEMON
GAME that gave birth to my creative side,
I used my creative head to try & stop the demons
to stem there overflowing tide.

Although I was heavily losing to THE DEMON GAME
my creative head was getting more & more use,
THE DEMON GAME was my creative heads training
ground it was homing its skills all throughout my abuse.
They say with every gift comes a curse they say they come hand in hand,
Was THE DEMON GAME my curse were
I so nearly made my final stand.
THE DEMON GAME gave birth to the gift of my
creative head yet it so nearly took my life away,
Which makes me even more grateful for life my
creative head & for just being here today.

MY LIFE'S DREAMS

What r your life's dreams & why does every
human being have dreams to hold onto,
Is it just human nature telling us these r things for the
future dreams you must try & follow through.
What if you believe in fate if you truly believe
your future has already been planned,
What then of dreams surly if you believe in
fate then dreams would be dammed.
I guess it's all down to the individual dreamers heart & head being
able 2 keep alive the knowledge of what they r dreaming for,
Some dreams may come easy others may land
you in an un winnable dog eat dog war.
One of my biggest dreams is to become a writer to help educate
the world of THE DEMON GAME & its deadly ways,
To show THE DEMON GAME is getting stronger now destroying
whole families no longer does it only go after 1 of strays.
I dream of meeting my perfect lady to become my lifelong wife,
I dream that my body has enough left in it to give me a long fruitful life.
I dream of a stable home children & grandchildren later on in life,
I hope I do meet that perfect lady for these dreams to come
true it would help to have by my side that perfect wife.
I don't dream for money or fortune nor do I dream for fame,
But I do dream for my small things to be kept close to keep the lights
on in what is the most important stage of my new life's game.
I dream that I keep becoming a more wiser loving caring open
minded man who this time listens to the best interests of his heart,
I dream that my closest loved ones are kept safe & r
with me to the end as they were at the start.
But most of all I dream that 1 day my soul will forgive the old & new me,
Forgive us for allowing all those permanent scares to
be left on the head & heart of the reel lee.
Then maybe just maybe it won't just be a dream of what I want for me,
Maybe that blissful day will come when my soul will fall
back in love with the real dreamer that is lee.

AFTERMATH

My day to day life is now living in the
aftermath of THE DEMON GAME,
A tiny piece of the old lee is the only thing to have
made it to the aftermath still the same.
I now have to pay back the heavy financial costs that
throughout THE DEMON GAME I done,
It seems that from THE DEMON GAME I am constantly on the run.
My cash situation isn't all that good with me
struggling to pay the weekly bills,
Just another twisted pieces of the aftermath of snorting
2 many lines of swallowing too many demon pills.
Bank loans credit & store cards rent council tax
there all adding up to a heavy toll,
At least I can truthfully say I feed my habit with my Owen cash
I am proud to be able to say to feed my habit I never stole.
But all these things r immaterial & I never allow them to get me down,
As I have always done I still somehow manage to get
the odd night here & there out on the town.
All that matters is that I am getting by & even now writing
the words getting by still comes as a slight shock,
Shocked that I did make it out especially when I was so sure I
had already over run the time I had left on its deadly clock.
But I can't complain because mentally & physically I am always
getting stronger this part of my life is going the right way,
And in time my debts will come down then no
longer will I have to always pay pay pay.
Lately I have been doing a lot of thinking about my future
it's probably the first time I have ever thought ahead,
It has amazed me what my head can do since its
switched its self back on after so many years being
overpowered exiled to the land of the living dead.

I have been thinking of what now to do with myself
what out of my life can I now make,
I know 1 of my biggest dreams is to become that writer I can
only hope this dream is one I am given a chance to take.
I would also like a chance to help other demon
game victims sort out there dark strife,
All I know is I no longer want to be this nobody in this nothing life.
I want to make myself a life that will make my mother proud,
I want to be able to shout I have made a difference
I want to be able to shout it clear & loud.

TAKE ME BY THE HAND

Slipping sliding falling into the soft gold drowning sand,
Raising my arm waiting for someone or
something to take me by the hand.
But when you put out your hand its only grasped by hands that
lead you astray they join you indulging in that deadly sin,
In this underprivileged west coast drugs usually always win.
In this west coast there is no were to go nothing to do but
plenty of cheap drugs that will take you by the hand,
Around these parts drugs r taken as a release they r
seen as the thing to pull you out of the sand.
When everybody around you is smoking weed snorting Charlie
popping pills it becomes hard to tell fact from fiction,
It's so hard to get away from your bad habits your sins
everything just seems to be part of one massive addiction.
The more drugs that r taken become the more that
r wanted the more they become needed,
Drugs r like the weeds in an overgrown garden so
overgrown it can never be fully weeded.
The soft gold sinking sand is the trap to the young & the cage to the old,
Once in it on a few make it out of the soft gold sinking sands evil mold.
When you come from such an underprivileged west
coast will mass unemployment ever rising crime rate
you quickly realize you are not alone in the sand,
Behind you there is a sea of drug dealers drug takers drug
abusers drug addicts all reaching for the same hand.

FORESEEN

Fourteen years ago to this very day is this life the 1 I
thought I would be living did this life I foresee,
No it is not this is truly not the life I thought would be for me.
Before I started taking drugs the Para's was
the only thing I ever wanted to be,
My father & grandfather were Para's it was the only life for me.
Then I started taking drugs & all of a sudden
there was a ? On what I was going to be,
All of a sudden the Para's was not the only life I could see.
I could never have foreseen that drugs would open my
mind to a whole new world a whole new way of life,
Never would I have been able to foresee THE DEMON
GAME with all its years of painful lonely dark strife.
I would never have foreseen that drugs were the
key needed to unlock my creative head,
Could I have foreseen that the gamble I would
take could have left me dead.
I could never have foreseen that I would be distend to
write all this poetry all these poems just to write,
I would never have foreseen that this long painful road
would have turned me into the man I am tonight.
I would never have foreseen that a long painful road would have
turned me into such a gifted young man with such an open mind,
At such a young age you don't realize that life sometimes
has to be very cruel b4 it can be kind.
Back then I could not have foreseen that if I didn't take
this road I wouldn't be the man I am today,
I could have turned out very bad the kind of person
from your life you try to keep far away.

So sitting right now thinking of the destruction all the mistakes
I still feel that I took the right path the right trail I did take,
And only in my unseen future will I find out if it has been a mistake.
But the? I cannot answer is if I could have foreseen all this
would I have taken this life would I have lead it this way,
Or back when I was a young & drug free would I have chosen
a different path would I have chosen to stay away.

UNEXPLAINABLE URGES

On a clear calm night you can look up & see an
unrivaled beauty that is the stars in the night sky,
Think back to the first astromenir who had the
unexplainable urge to map them why??.
What causes the unexplainable urge in people to come
up with something that is the first of its kind,
The unexplainable urge that courses through their body
until they have a crystal clear image of it in their mind.
That person has just had an unexplainable urge that
no 1 else on the planet has had before,
Do they realize what has just happened to them
or is it later when it begins once more.
Are the unexplainable urges already there & 1 of them
from your mind you have just managed to recover,
Or r these unexplainable urges sent from a higher form
of conscious that we have not yet discovered.
Are these unexplainable urges sparked by situations you encounter
during life things that happen at a certain time in a certain place,
Are they sparked by something someone says
by a strange look on a strangers face.
What why or who is it that chooses the individual
to have that unexplainable urge,
And why does that individual know how to decipher that explosive surge.
Why do you get the unexplainable urge to keep that deciphered
picture clear in your mind as a constant thought,
Without knowing it you have become the creator of something
that others may have spent their life's waiting for always sought.
You r now the sol possessor of an unexplainable urge the
first of its kind & with it comes the ? What to do,
Do you dismiss it as just another emotion you cannot explain or do you
embrace it give it life let the world know this creation belongs to you.

When you think about it so much in life is
just 1 big unexplainable mystery,
The only things I can explain r those I already
know from my life's history.
So what was the unexplainable urge in me that
decided writing would become my realize,
How did that unexplainable urge know that only when writing
would I find that much needed tiny bit of inner peace.

TAKERS WISDOM

As we get older we r suppose to get wiser they say wisdom comes with age,
What happens when most of your life's years
were spent in a drugged up rage.
When you take a drug it opens doors in your head
doors that once opened you cannot close,
All of a sudden you see the world in a whole different
way is this part wisdom this is the question I pose.
As soon as that first drug hits your system it opens doorways that
allow you to see & feel in a way you have never experienced before,
Your body mind & soul r now experiencing thoughts emotions &
feelings like no others & your head is always left wanting more.
Things you've always taken for granted run through your head &
(BANG) for the first time you see them in a whole different light,
Love friendship memories all running through your head you really
don't want to come down to see the end of this life changing night.
Without drugs to open the doorways you would never be
able to experience the feelings thoughts & overpowering
emotions that r exploding through your veins,
Beware because once you have tasted this experience you will
look back at normal life & realize its basic boring & plain.
But as any wise drug taker will tell you if you go overboard drugs will
open dark doorways that no human soul should be made or have to feel,
With a blink of an eye they will take your life from you make
you so week all you will be able to do is beg & kneel.
If your r sensible & stay as an occasional drug taker
then in time the wisdom you may find,
If you slip & become a drug abuser then overwhelming
destruction will be the only doorway opened to your mind.

All the wisdom I have gained though my years of drug taking makes me
say to non drug takers don't take them it's not a place you need to go,
You have never experienced these thoughts feelings or
emotions so it's not something you don't need to no.
Through drugs wisdom does not come overnight
does not come easy you don't get it for free,
Overwhelming destruction to the body heart mind & soul is its price
this is something non drug takers ever feel only through takers see.

MY DEMON HALF

Over the next 4 poems I am going to try & explain what its like to be me,
My demon half, my creative head, my alter ego, the
real me 4 sides you have to individually see.
I'll start with my demon half the strongest of them all
the one that lives within me day after day,
The first time I took a drug it was born in me and its
now here for what seems to be an everlasting stay.
I have this demon stuck in me as if with the strongest glue,
It's the only part of me that I struggle to control it still
occasionally does to me whatever it wants to do.
It has only 1 goal 1 purpose to try & get me
back into a life of drugged up rage,
This is what it does to me if it's allowed to slip out of its cage.
It's the only part of me that still wants my old
life somehow it still feels the need,
Its my raging demon half that sometimes I still have to occasionally feed.
If I occasionally feed my demon half it leaves me
to get on with a life of relative plain,
If I don't feed my demon half it bursts out dragging me
back towards the dark addictive demon game.
The only way I know how to keep control of it is to occasionally
feed to keep happy my destructive dark other half,
If I don't feed him he could still easily be the end of me he's still strong
enough to nail my other 3 sides to LUSEFARS burning wooden staff.

MY CREATIVE HEAD

Now onto my creative head which is getting
stronger day by day always stronger,
Gone r the days when I struggled to control my gift those days r no longer.
You see in the beginning my gift would just burst into my
head & I would have to write as fast as my pen would go,
I lost so much writing in the early days because I
couldn't slow it down at that time in my head I didn't
have the knowledge needed I didn't have the no.
I would wake up in the middle of the night with sometimes just a
few words in my head so I would write a little reminder note,
And months later when writing a poem I would
realize why that verse was wrote.
It was chaos with nothing in order everything mixed up & out of place,
Everything was bursting in & out of my head as
if it was some kind of mad chaotic race.
But the more time I spent writing with my gift the more I
began to understand the ins and outs of my creative head,
Now if need be I can slow it down speed it up no longer
am I awoke with a thousand thoughts in my bed.
The only thing about my creative head that I
don't control is when it is time to write,
For I have a gift not a talent it chooses its time
sometimes morning sometimes late at night.

THE REAL ME

And now to the real me a person that only a few
have had the privilege to meet to see,
99.9% of the people that no me have never
met or even know of the real me.
The real me is loving respectful trustworthy but most of all really shy,
And the worst thing is shy people don't fit in 2 this world
from my Owen experience I know is not a lie.
No one realizes the confidence is shy people is fragile & week,
Every1 just looks at shy people as loaners or some kind of freak.
This big bad world doesn't give shy people the time of day &
most live out lonely life's filled with heart break & pain,
If you were just to give them the time of day u will realize
they r the best friends you could ever meet or gain.
Shy people will be your friend for life they
will make your wellbeing a must,
You will see they r a friend that with your very life you could trust.
I knew that if I didn't hide my shyness this world would leave
me behind to the heart break & pain of life alone,
So the real me I hid & in its place put out a stronger alter ego a clone.

MY ALTER EGO

And last but not least to my alter ego that all my
friends & family know & have come to love,
An alter ego I created so perfect that it fits over the real me like a glove.
I created my alter ego to protect the real me
from the world and its deadly lowers,
An alter ego to try and make sure the real lee was
kept clean uncorrupted and 1oo% pure.
An alter ego that has stood strong even through
the demon game with all its evil strife,
An alter ego big enough strong enough to fight for the real me in this life.
I created an alter ego so strong that for the 21 years
that it has been by my side only for 6 months did it let
the demons of drugs through to the real me,
But in those 6 months they done so much damage to
assure I would never again feel the 100% pure lee.
I can't complain my alter ego is still in tacked it took the
brink of the demon game hid it & fought it for so long,
But in the end even for my alter ego for a short
time the demons were too strong.
My alter ego is still here to get me by I use it every day,
Life is much easier when I use my alter ego so
this is the way it will forever stay.
My demon half, creative head, real me, alter ego, all these
sides in one broken body heart mind & soul,
The strangest thing is these 4 sides make me 1 by simply keeping me hole.

CONDEMNED

My body has been condemned to THE DEMON GAME
& the place where it came from called hell,
The unseen damage my body sustained during THE DEMON GAME
not knowing how much or how bad these r things I can't yet tell.
My heart has been condemned to mother earth there's 2
many missing pieces to try & get it into heaven,
I only hope that what is left of my heart will one day heal
to love again I pray this is a chance my heart is given.
My mind well it can't be condemned its spent too much time traveling
through all 3 sides' real life THE DEMON GAME & its living hell,
Were my mind will end up your guess is as good
as mine am left thinking oh well.
My alter ego has been condemned to a life with me,
In this big bad world I couldn't live without it that
would be a life I would never want to see.
My demon half has been condemned to an uncertain
future were it may or may not survive,
But for the time being my demon half is most certainly alive.
And my soul well it has also been condemned to a life with me,
I hope in time it will forgive & once again I
will be whole we will be all lee.
And my creative head well it has been condemned to a life of
trying to put into words things that can't usually be spoken,
To get wiser & stronger & I know my creative
head has become my life's lucky token.
So what of the real me what life has it been condemned to will it
continue to live in the shadows of my other more powerful sides,
Only to get out on the rare occasions to pick up the pieces of
my world that has begun to float away on life's strong tides.
Or has the real me got a new roll in my roller coaster of a life,
Has the real me got a more prominent roll to stand up &
be counted in what is mostly its condemned life.

INSIDE THE WALLS

Dysfunctional souls, depression, destruction, death,
loneliness, pain, & vast empty dark spaces,
These r the only things you will find inside the walls of THE
DEMON GAME these r the only things that were granted places.
If you r outside then you have nothing to fear from THE DEMON
GAME none of its evil can escape the walls not even the smallest sin,
And no matter how hard you try you will never breach the walls
unless you r stupid enough to take a drug & invite yourself in.
So let this be a warning to all stupid enough to invite there selves
in once there you cannot leave the walls only work one way,
Even if you beat your addiction inside the walls
emotionally apart of you will forever stay.
Once inside the only way out is the way you came in
take a drug & you are given a pass outside the walls
but it only lasts as long as you can stay high,
How ironic the more passes you use to go out into the light
the darker it is when you return because another little
piece of you was given in the name of drugs to die.
Yes at first there seems to be no light & it is as scary as
hell but you must be man enough to take responsibility for
the life you put inside the walls you must have the guts to
stand up in the darkness & say I take all the blame,
There is nothing more pathetic than a drug abuser blaming
the world (NEWSFLASH) there's only one way to find
light inside the walls Owen up to your Owen shame.
I have the balls to ad might that my past mistakes have
left a Hugh part of me trapped inside the walls & yes
sometimes through the darkness it's hard to see,
But I am no longer afraid of the dark & I will make a better
life for myself even if I have to get my physical body to
push the emotional walls along with the rest of me.

Look at me now am so used to having a Hugh piece of me trapped
inside the walls that unless tomorrow brings a situation where I
need a certain missing emotion I don't even notice they are gone,
But if tomorrow does bring that situation it's always a killer to be
reminded that inside me things are so very emotionally wrong.
If you want to live to see any light inside the walls you
must live by one simple rule damage limitation don't
bring more darkness to an already dark place,
If you bring more you your self will disappear your name your very
existence will vanish into the darkness without so much as a trace.
And here it comes the twisted irony is the same mistake that
put you inside the walls becomes the only short term way out
but only if you are willing to pay the heavy emotional cost,
A little piece of advice from a old wise head live inside
the walls without using the passes they will only grant you
access to being a step closer to a life that is lost.
Ironically my soul destroying life taking creation that is the
dark addictive demon game somehow occasionally allows me
to light up the darkness even inside the walls I am granted a
tiny flicker of remembrance of a life that used to shine,
At least I still have the balls not to lower myself & use the world as an
excuse all blame lies in the reason that my demon half could not be
controlled by a broken soldier who's fault WELL ITS ALL MINE.

EMOTIONALLY APART SOLDIER

When the moment comes & finally to yourself you willingly
admit that a war fought in hell has consumed your life &
its scares r the only expressions left on your face,
The very moment your war with THE DEMON GAME begins
you become part of the life against deaths unwinnable race.
The longer a soldier spends fighting THE DEMON
GAME the further they are pushed from real life from the
rest of the world you become emotionally apart,
The pieces of you that don't make it through the destruction
leave you an emotionally damaged soldier instead of the fully
functioning emotional human being you were at the start.
Now everyday you sit back & watch as the rest of the world
takes everything & everyone for granted they don't realize
how good they have it being emotionally pure,
You have become a broken soldier emotionally apart
from the rest so these things you pick up on because
not so long ago those things were happily yours.
You go to sleep & awake with emptiness a void inside you
that no man woman child or even religion can fill,
The emptiness is caused by the parts of you that did not make it
through the battles fought with your liquid plant powder or pills.
You are an emotionally apart soldier trying to fight your
way through the war that is life a war fueled by the
rawest emotions that to so many r never seen,
So many soldiers r lost because they feel they don't have the
emotional weapons needed to fight a war against an enemy
that already has the upper hand the rub of the green.
The only weapon we emotionally apart soldiers now have
is the knowledge & power of a well tuned head a fortress of
wisdom & strength that is our supercharged minds,
From within the walls of your fortress you can take time
to study the map of life you will have time to choose
your path pick a direction & follow the signs.

For if a soldier loses control over his army of emotions they will
become his biggest threat inevitably he will deal himself the
fatal blow that will bring with it the end to his war of life,
Without the weapon of a wise powerful mind any army of
emotions is useless all they become is the hand that deals
the killer blow by sticking in twisting the knife.
I became an emotionally apart soldier because my family split up
when I was only young I couldn't control my army of emotions
as they dragged me into the battle with the soul destroying
demon game weaker, outnumbered, out gunned, my army
should have been annihilated faster than a fleeting glance,
But with what can only be described as a miracle some
pieces of my army hung on to witness that biblical night
when reinforced with faith this soldier was given a army
that could that would that stood a fighting chance.
So to all the other emotionally apart soldiers your r not alone you have
become part of a new breed, a new brotherhood of soldiers with different
ways different weapons from the vast army of the emotional same,
Use the wisdom & strength of your mind trust it to lead you
safely through the battles that lie ahead in this mentally
emotionally & physically crippling life's game.
For me the battle with the demon game is over but in
my heart mind body & soul it will forever remain in the
knowledge that I did not fight an enemy I fought myself &
lost possession of my soul I let the demon game take nearly
everything from me swallowed by its dark drowning sands,
But God has shown me a place where all damage is fixed were
all soldiers r welcome were all must become equal before you
r aloud to enter his almighty soldiers promised land.
But for the time being here I must stay to record the ongoing
destruction I must stay to do GODS wile with on my soul a hidden
curse that may never allow me to get to his promised land,
This emotionally apart soldier must rely on his gifted mind
to see him through the battles that will decide wither
he goes to the devil or wither with his new brotherhood
of soldiers he is finally in peace allowed to stand.

TURNING THE TIDE

Do you think it's too late to turn the tide on drugs
do you think drugs have dug in too deep,
Will we always keep losing loved ones will always
have only that little time left to weep.
Nowadays it seems that every young person you now
is taking drugs or at some point they had,
And it's not just the young ones the older as just as bad.
Does this drug taking society want to turn the
tide do they themselves want to turn,
Do they all realize that in their heads there are only
certain things you can allow drugs to burn.
How many more deaths through drugs will it take to
make them realize it's time to turn the tide,
How many more lives ruined before they realize
to come back to the sensible side.
Do they realize that the next drug they take could be the one to finally
brakes them the one that won't allow them to turn back the tide,
Do they realize when it happens no matter what they do they
will never be able to come back to the sensible side.
Are you sitting back right now realizing its already to
late the door in front of you has been locked,
And the demons in your head have been counted set free well stocked.
What will you do now when you've realized
your chance has gone it's too late,
Now you're sliding into a life of self destruction that's your new fate.
And now well on your way to self destruction you see in
your head the chance you had to turn the tide,
Realizing you shouldn't have been that little sheep and followed
you should have been the wolf & turned to the other side.
In every drug taker there is a wolf & a sheep,
Will you be the wolf & turn the tide or will you are the
sheep & only have that little time left to weep.

TIME

There is a question I find myself pondering over
quite a lot nowadays a question about time,
Is my life vastly running out of it like old cliff's
crumbling because there made of soft lime.
Have i got the time to see an old age or is it to run out b4 is this my fate,
How much time you have left in life is like the meaning
you never know the answer till it's too late.
If there is 1 thing I don't believe in it that your life's time
& story have been wrote & set b4 you are born,
I believe your life's time & story are written & lengthen by the decisions
you make that's why over some of your decisions you can end up so torn.
I know that when my life is coming close to its end I
will look back & realize that even my bad experiences
where precise they were all part of my time,
I will ask did I use my time wisely did I spend too
many years living a life of drugs & grime.
As long as I have time left I am going to live it
to the full sensible & as good as I can,
I will try to get THE DEMON GAME published so
it may help others & maybe I will be remembered for
something good instead of just that crazy ass man.
Because THE DEMON GAME consumed my life for so many painful
years I now fully appreciate how precise time really is for lee,
I now no to enjoy & embrace every second b4 there is no time left for me.
Every year month day hour minute second is precise
time that is constantly ticking away,
Time is something I cannot turn back so what's left of it
I will live to the full right up 2 my very last day.
Evan as I write my time is ever ticking away
for time stands still for no man,
This is why I never look too far into the future
time is something no 1 can plan.

I live from day 2 day never planning ahead
trying not to dwell 2 much on my past'
It doesn't matter how much time we get it's never
enough & it most certainly will not last.
If you spend 2 much time dwelling on your past planning your
future you will miss your present the time you have right now,
You will only end up asking yourself where did
my time go what when where & how.
How much time any1 gets in life is something not
even the world's smartest scientists could call,
Is the damage drugs have done to me going 2 shorten my
time will it be sooner rather than later when I fall.

DRAWING A BLANK

My alter ego is blessed with the gift of the gab the
ability to make any1 at anytime laugh,
At party's I step up on2 my stage take control of the
room no matter how many r there or who's gaff.
I am the joker of the pack always using my comedy
2 hide the fact that I am really quite shy,
I have become so good I can have any1 in stitches
without braking sweat I don't even have 2 try.
I can pretty much talk my way in & out of any situation bad or good,
I hit them with a barrage of fast & furious jokes engulfing their
attention this leaves me free 2 control the rooms mood.
So why the hell is it that when trying to chat up any girl
I like these supers gift of the gab draws a blank,
It's like my words turn in2 useless ammunition
that I am firing at an impenetrable tank.
Wait a minute this is the boy that always without fail has an
answer 4 everything so why is there now nothing in my head,
Just clocked the look on the girls face because without
any warning the conversation stopped dead.
Why is it that with ease I can have any woman laughing all
night long laughing so hard the tears stream down there face,
But as soon as I try & cross that mental barrier & attempt to chat her
up my gift of the gab leaves me & fucks off to a whole different place.
What happens to make this super confident free
flowing comedian 4get his tactics 4get his ploy,
In a blink of an eye I turn in2 a confused speechless
empty headed embarrassed young boy.
The harder I try to find something to say the more I
draw a blank & the quicker time stands still,
My thoughts frozen in the moment like motionless
blades on an old disused wind mill.

I have friends that can take home a different girl every weekend they
say all they have to do is whisper sweet nothings in there ear,
To them pulling is always easy straight 4ward crystal clear.
They say lee its easy just tell them what they want to hear,
But when I open my mouth my head draws a blank
& silence is the only thing to fill their ears.
I guess I am just doomed to not be able to see when
or if a girl is interested even when they are pointed
out 2 me I always seem to miss the signs,
Once the mental barrier is crossed I draw a blank which makes it
impossible to read what is clearly written between the lines.

IRONY

Irony is knowing I am a dyslexic poet trying 2
describe 2 the world his drug addicted hell,
Irony is knowing a demon spawned of those drugs gave birth 2 my
creative head my alter ego the overwhelming destruction 2 the real
me & yes this story has most certainly been a hard one 2 tell.
Irony is knowing that from birth against each other
my 4 split personality's have been raging an all out
mental war a endless emotional battle,
Irony is knowing in TURNING THE TIDE I was the wolf yet I have
ended up in the poison where I can't seem to end this ongoing tattle.
Irony is knowing that 2 other people's lives I was always known as
the fixer saying the right thing at the right time doing what was
needed without being asked always being there as if I had never left
looking out 4 those who for their lives never took time 2 look,
Irony is knowing that the life that needed fixing the most I could not
save & all that's left of it is what's written inside the pages of this book.
Irony is knowing just how much damage the drugs where doing
knowing what had 2 be done 2 fix the life I could not save,
Irony is knowing from the 4 created none will survive my endless taking
of wrong chances hence why we continue 2 hand dig our own grave.
Irony is knowing u r your sworn savor who is
hell bent on total self destruction,
Irony is knowing with 8 feet 4 mind sets 2 opposite goals
finding that happy life will need a miracle construction.
Irony is knowing that GOD himself made a point
of personally telling me he is on my side,
Irony is knowing your demon is so dark that LUCIFER
himself has no interest in turning the tide.
Irony is knowing u r 2 blame for every fracture every brake in your heart
every missing emotion every little problem u created in your head,
Irony is knowing u did read the set of instructions &
still allowed yourself 2 b so easily miss lead.

Irony is knowing every morning u will awake
2 your own self created shame,
Irony is knowing no matter how hard u look
u will never find someone 2 blame.
Irony is knowing u spent all day looking 4 a pencil because
the task u had required u not 2 leave a permanent mark,
Irony is knowing when u came 2 write this poem there was
not a pen 2 b seen another 1 of irony's upside down facts.
Irony is knowing that through my self destruction I will never
find my missing link i keep drawing a blank I no longer posses the
confidence 2 make myself meet that perfect lady 2 become my wife,
Irony is knowing that irony its self has become the
meaning to the description of your life.

SPECIAL GIRL

Do you think I will ever meat a special girl that will be able to live
with the knowledge of what the demon game has done to lee,
A special girl that will be able to love me as me.
A special girl that will be able to understand
the knowledge of the demon game,
A special girl that will stick by my side that will stand by my name.
A special girl that won't be afraid of the demon game that
will realize its something I have already come through,
A special girl to realize I have already tightened the screw.
A special girl that won't think I am nothing but a freak,
A special girl to realize I am no longer week.
A special girl that won't make me feel like scum for
what I wrote on those cold painful nights,
A special girl to realize THE DEMON GAME was
something I had to tell I was forced to write.
A special girl to realize I have already made a fresh start,
A special girl to realize all that's left of the demon
game is locked deep in my head & heart.
A special girl who will help me overcome my fears,
A special girl who will understand why I have
shed so many painful empty tears.
A special girl to realize THE DEMON GAME could
happen to any person & I have not been the only 1,
To realize underneath it all there's a loving caring trustworthy
person from whom she does not need to run.
A special girl to see the good in me as if the real lee she already new,
To realize I am different only because of what I have come through.
A special girl that will be able to love the person I now am,
A special girl that will add to my life love stability
& a much needed sense of calm.

A special girl that can understand what it is I
am wanting & trying so hard to be,
To see that all I want is to be loved to have
a special girl to care about me.
Do you think I will ever meat this special girl do you
think she could be waiting out there for me,
Do you think there is a special girl out there that
would want to be the other half of Lee.

SO CALLED FRIENDS

An essential part of any human beings existence is
friends also known as chums mates crew,
But as the years go by most of these friends fade
away into associates you once new.
I have seen so many friends come & go over the years
ones that have faded in & out of my bubble,
I have seen too many turn crewel on me bringing
me nothing but hurt & trouble.
I saw to many so called friends turn on me when I
was going through THE DEMON GAME,
So called friends that turned on me bringing with them
more hurt & shame to my already broken name.
I thought the meaning of friends were people
who stick by you through thin & thick,
I didn't think it meant they were only there when
you were down to give you an extra kick.
Even still to this day some of these so called friends still look
down there noises at me like I am a piece of shit on the street,
Looking to say they would not use me to so much as wipe their feet.
The thing that gets me the most is that I did not
hurt or offend any of these so called chums,
So why did these people turn against me I can't
work it out no matter what way I do sums.
But I'll be honest about these so called friends I could not give a
fuck I have never over them missed so much as a wink of sleep,
There just people I now wish I didn't meat.
So I think I'll be more careful how I choose my friends your
always better to look 4 the ones who r good at heart,
If they r good at heart never will you have a problem
with them not at the finish nor at the start.

TRUE FRIENDS

An essential part of my existence is my true
friends also known as Bubba's crew,
These r the friends that through everything have
stood by me they r my very special few.
These r the friends that when the demon game was destroying
me were always there every time I called their names,
These r the ones that backed me up even in
my darkest times of self shame.
These r the friends that with me were never scared to shed a tear,
These r the friends that were standing behind me when I
was looking into the face of my overwhelming fears.
These r the friends that have never judged me on
anything I have done all throughout my life,
These r the friends that were willing to stand in front of me
to protect me from my overwhelming drug afflicted strife.
These r the friends that if they could have would have
changed places with me to take my overwhelming pain,
These r the friends that all throughout the insanity
done everything they could to keep me sane.
These were the friends that were willing to listen to the demon
game as I wrote it piece by piece pushing me to finish to the end,
They r the friends that were there before r still here
today now that's the definition of true friends.
These r the true friends that tell me I am gifted not a freak,
These r the friends that show me I am strong not week.
To these true friends I owe a debt I can never repay,
These r the true friends that say I owe them
nothing because that is there way.
So to Frank G Dinger Bal T Ryan Patie & Paul,
Straight from the heart your true friend lee loves & thanks you all.
(Frank-Frank William Roberts) (G-Garth Turnbull) (Sean
Devlin) (Dinger-Stephen Bell) (Bal-Alistair Cairnie)
(T-Mark McMahon) (Ryan-Ryan Ian White) (Patie-
Craig Paterson) (Paul-Paul Philip Samuel Simpson)

LUCKY FRIEND

I had a dream last night about an incident that happened
a good few years ago in my old party flat,
It's the scariest thing I have ever seen so I'll tell you of this
incident & now 2gether in time we will go back.
Sitting back having a laugh with 1 of my best m8ts T,
T laughing at the usual crazy shit said by me.
All of a sudden T drops back in2 the chair,
Eye's shut so I can no longer see his laughing stair.
He starts to vibrate like some1 is pumping unlimited
amounts of electricity through his veins,
Foam coming from both sides of his mouth then blood
now I see this is no joke my m8t T is in real pain.
I jump up shouting T T are you ok,
Seeing him vibrate & thinking T is dead on this day.
I manage to prise his jaws open & pull his tongue from his throat,
Thinking 2 myself don't you die on me T don't you dare give up the goat.
Saying T don't you dare leave your mother & brothers to grieve,
Shouting T breathe T breathe.
Finally he stops shaking & 2 the kitchen i make my brake,
Knowing not 2 leave him 2 long 1 of my best m8ts life is still at stake.
I rush back to T & get a damp cold cloth 2 his head,
He starts 2 come around a little more leaving
me 2 thank GOD he's not dead.
He is looking up at me with a look on his face that
says what the fuck r you doing to me,
He doesn't realize that I have just saved his life
this part 2 him was impossible 2 see.
He then starts 2 talk mumbo jumbo which is foreign 2 my ears,
At least I no he is alive & it gives me a little
second to wipe back my tears.

Now he is sitting up without the slightest clue
2 what he has just come through,
But the strange thing is he suddenly turns 2 me &
say's I would be dead if it wasn't for you.
Then the realization kicks in of what has just happened to T,
T has no memory but that night will never fade will
always be crystal clear in the memory of lee.
This 1 is dedicated to 1 of my best friends Mark
McMahon the turtle a.k.a T...xx

HAPPILY ENCASED

Looking around at everything happily sitting here
encased in my little world of excited dreams,
Some of my friends r hear encased with me in our
little world protected by its tight seems.
Encased in our world where everything is fine & always sweet,
When we r encased we glide & the whole world sits at our feet.
Encased in our world were the conversations r deep
& meaningful packed with nothing but good,
We all dissect the conversations rant & rave time
always flies when we r encased in this mood.
Encased in a world without grief pain anger or fights,
In our encased world we only allow piece love loud music & bright lights.
Your head & body feel as if it's the first time
they have truly been aloud 2 live,
Your heart & soul have a blinding glow encased
in our world of give give give.
Encased 4 the night in a world that makes you feel
as if no wrong will ever be again done,
Your only wish is that all your friends could be here instead of just some.
Encased in this overwhelming piece love & happiness always leaves
you with the thought of being un encased back 2 real life,
Back 2 were nightmares come true in a world filled with dark strife.
But 4 now you're still encased so that thought just
keeps slipping to the back of your mind,
For we r still in our blissful world where we
all meet 2 be encased & unwind.
Encased in a world with its own time it's like looking
at life from the top of the tallest tree,
This is why we over look the destruction 2 the head
body mind & soul we are willing 2 trade that for a few
hours of being happily encased in our world of E.
Once you have been encased most go back 4 more
putting the destruction 2 the back of their mind,
In this long hard life ironically 4 some of us it's the only
place we feel we can go 2 truly mentally unwind.

MORALS

What has happened to morals respect & trust,
Not so long ago to lead life these things were a must.
But not 2day for the whole world has been turned upside down,
Lies cheating back stabbing its happening in every town.
The younger generation that has no respect,
It's got so far that no longer can the older generation this problem correct.
The men & women who so easily cheat on their other half,
Not so long ago for that kind of behavior they
would have been burned at the staff.
Liars who take it upon them self's 2 destroy the lives of others,
Life's that were created with the hope of happiness by fathers & mothers.
Back stabbers whose only pleasure is to see others in pain,
There to put people on2 the dark side of the game.
Not so long ago there was a society based on love respect trust & morals,
But somewhere along the years this society went wrong
& now all this society does is with its self quarrel.
Yes there was a blissful time when morals were all throughout mankind,
Now those times are only left in the memory of the older mind.
For morals trust love & respect r being bread out of the human race,
They r being bread out at an unbelievable pace.
If its like this now what will it be like in 3 generations to come,
Will there be such a thing as a stable home for the
many or will it only be 4 the privileged some.
So I sit back & ask you have humanity gone
beyond the point where we can save,
Or is this no morale human race only digging its own grave.
There is only the few in so many that still have morals trust & respect,
These few have been put on the endangered species list
they have become something we need to protect.

THE CHILD WITHIN

Can you remember way back 2 when you were a child,
Playing out your back door with your friends running free running wild.
Back 2 a time when you had nothing on your
mind but play & play some more,
Back 2 a time when even throwing stones would
amuse you nothing was a bore.
Running around with your friends laughing
& screaming in2 the youthful air,
Running around laughing & screaming without a care.
Saying things that have no meaning showing off 2 all your friends,
This life is all you can see at the end of your youthful lens.
The only thing that bothers you is when you are
shouted in b4 the day turns to night,
All you want to do is stay out playing in that youthful frenzied flight.
You live a life of total bliss lived in your little youthful bubble,
Nothing but youthful fun can get through no hurt no trouble.
Running at the front of the pack shouting quick quick every1 follow me,
Those were truly the happiest days of your life its
only when they've passed can this you see.
Every day is just fun everyday you're out having the time of your life,
Do you enjoy your youth so much because next you are introduced
to the real world with things like loneliness hurt & strife.
When you are a child you don't have the knowledge the understanding
to see any further than the end of your youthful sight,
You don't know that with a blink of an eye you will be in the
real world with its overpowering allures strength & might.
You are a blissful innocent young child with
nothing on your mind but fun,
Abilities to the knowledge needed to stay on the bumpy road
of life imprinted with the knowledge to crash & burn.
Often the child within me wishes I could go back to
those care free days when I could run free & wild,
Now more than ever I truly believe if GOD
loves you he takes you as a child.

BIRD OF CHANCE

Some1 once told me life is something U make,
If U want something bad enough it will B yours 2 take.
But this is not true that's just the talk of the already privileged
1'ns making it out the way 2 us they think it should seem,
If this was true every human would have everything they
have ever wanted everything from their wildest dreams.
There R so many talented people out there that want
dream & try for a better life so bad but will never get
the chance 2 make their dreams come true,
Never there at the right time never heard never discovered as if
the BIRD OF CHANCE had over there had head just flown.
The BIRD OF CHANCE will only choose a few in so many 1 in
a 1,000,000 that is there at the right time in the right place,
That is why so many of the good gifted artists R never discovered no
1 will ever know their story no 1 will ever recognize there face.
It's always easy for the 1'ns the bird of chance has already chosen 2
sit & say if U want something bad enough there is always a way,
But the hard hitting truth is 999 out of a 1000 artists
will never make it out of there unknown life's not
through choice it's just were there destined 2 stay.
If U R sitting reading this then it probably means by
the BIRD OF CHANCE I have been chosen I have
been given that 1 in a 1,000,000 lucky break,
If U R not sitting reading this U will never know that
THE BIRD OF CHANCE has passed me by & to the
pile another unknown artists life has become fate.
If truth B told chances R I will end up with all the other passed
over artists in the graveyard of the gifted a place that up until
now I have only ever looked at with a quick glance,
But I will keep hoping & praying that maybe just maybe
I will B seen by the BIRD OF CHANCE.

Most of the truly special beautiful warm gifted people of this
world will never get the chance 2 truly for fill their potential
B discovered by this world they will never B known,
They had just never been on any of the paths that
the BIRD OF CHANCE had flown.
BIRD OF CHANCE is dedicated 2 all the truly gifted artists who will
never get that lucky break needed 2 share their gift with this world.

HOPEFUL

It's been hard sitting here writing these feelings 2 u,
Talking about these deep dark feelings is
something most people find hard 2 do.
About me I have just described my second life everything
from my smallest feeling to my biggest tears,
U don't have a clue how hard it is to spill on2
paper your life & its worst fears.
Not knowing if people will understand from where I am trying to come,
or is THE DEMON GAME only understood by
the few by the open minded some.
Hopeful that this will get across the message
2 at least 1 soul who is in need,
hopeful that in others it will destroy THE DEMON GAMES seed.
Hopeful that i have been able to stop the demons being able to unwind,
Hopeful that i have been able to save at least 1 persons mind.
Hopeful that someday some1 will turn around a say THE
DEMON GAME is the best they have ever read,
Hopeful my ears will hear them say it b4 i am dead.
Hopeful that THE DEMON GAME won't just end up
as something people will use against me to taunt,
Hopeful that THE DEMON GAME will make the impact i want.
Hope people will read so far in2 THE DEMON
GAME they will forget 2 blink,
Hopeful they will realize about drugs they must rethink.
Hopeful that people who haven't taken a drug will
now have a little understanding about THE DEMON
GAME they will now have a little no,
Hopeful they will realize that THE DEMON GAME
is somewhere virgin minds should not go.
Hopeful that the poor souls that r in THE DEMON GAME will
realize to give it up & in there Owen right become a star,
Hopeful in reading this u will find out who u r.

Hopeful that the world will sit up & listen,
Hopeful that i have made a few hearts glisten.
Not knowing if everything i have wrote has been in vain,
Knowing that so far all it has done is ease my Owen pain.
Hopeful that this will catch 1 of the publishers eye's,
Knowing that without the publishers THE
DEMON GAME will pass the world bye.

ROLLING THE DICE

I have already rolled the dice through childhood which
was lived out on my paradise island far away,
that was the first side of a 4 sided game which is life
that was the side where i wanted to stay.
Then it was on2 the second side of 4 & i must have rolled
the dice clean of the board & somehow missed a go,
on the second side came THE DEMON GAME the
second side seemed 2 b so long & painfully slow.
Now i have turned on2 the 3rd side of 4 & on this
side i must roll the dice at there very best,
because on this side i am chasing my life's dreams &
putting the gift of my creative head to its biggest test.
I must b careful & on this most important side roll the
dice perfect i don't want to over or under throw,
this roll will decide my dreams & which direction they will go.
I must strongly believe have faith that i can control the
dice & get my dreams 2 where i want them 2 b,
if only the outcome of this throw was there in front of me 2 see.
On this 3rd side of 4 i must follow up everything
with commitment passion & fire,
everything i do on this side of my life's game will have 2
b backed up with hunger & stack loads of desire.
If on this side i don't give 110% my life's dreams
don't have a chance of coming true,
i must b mentally prepared to give my all i must
b ready 2 do whatever it is i have 2 do.
Fingers crossed so far on this 3rd side things have been
going great or 2 me thats the way it seems,
even if the dice can't get me there i'll find some other way
for i won't i will not give up on my life's dreams.

 CHANCES

No matter what religion color creed rich poor
lower middle or upper classes,
You will all at some point make have or b given chances.
Some chances r given 2 people 2 allow them 2
make for there self or others a better life,
Some chances will make u nervous like when a man
is on 1 knee asking his lady 2 become his wife.
Some people through persistence determination or
hard work will forge there owen chances,
Some u will have time 2 think over others will
pass u faster than fleeting glances.
Sometimes out of no where u will have a chance 2
take its up 2 u wither u do or wither u don't,
Impulsive people will take every chance unlike the
people who play life safe take a chance they won't.
I used 2 b well known for my impulsive living i would take any &
every chance that came along evin if i new it was destined 2 fail,
I was so impulsive chances r i would have lay in my
coffin & let u hammer in the last nail.
Ironically the only chance i should have took was always there but
i wasn't brave enough or man enough 2 take the chance & fight,
The saddest thing is i was only taking every other chance in the
hope that 1 of them would make everything in my life right.
There is some consolation in knowing i have not been the only one 2
have taken the wrong chances in knowing i am not the only mug,
But there is no consolation in knowing that over & over i kept taking
the same wrong chance every time i have took or taken a drug.

I don't no why but some1 or something somewhere has saw fit
to give me a chance 2 come good given me a chance 2 become
something better than ant thing i ever thought i could b,
I am amazed that such a chance would b given 2
some1 as undeserving as little old me.
Up until now every chance ive had 2 better or make something
of my life i have screwed up wasted or never took,
So this is my chance to put away my drug takers bible & finally make
something pure & good 2 insert in2 my life's ever expanding book.

THE END

Now i thank u for reading what i had 2 tell 2 the end,
I hope u r thinking shit hot i hope that's where ur head i did send.
So now this is truly the end of my demon game
& 2 u i am saying my goodbye's,
Everything i have wrote has come from my
heart & soul 2 u i have wrote no lies.
Will i ever write a follow up 2 THE DEMON
GAME i could say yes or theres no way,
Maybe THE DEMON GAME was a 1 off & thats the way it should stay.
Now u no as much about me as my friends & foes,
Yet i no nothing of u nothing of your highs or lows.
So now i have come 2 the point where about THE
DEMON GAME i have nothing left 2 write,
Hopefully in the future our heads will once
again meet u never no they might.
Although our paths will probably never cross u will probably
remain a stranger 2 me right up 2 the day i am dead,
The strangest thing is now u have read my DEMON GAME
a tiny piece of me will always live on in your head.